Praise for

Siu's practical and simple methods of Qi (energy) contain the power to revolutionize our modern approach to mental and emotional health. A game changer. Siu's unique method of stopping conditioned thought patterns so you can find your way back to your inner peace is brilliant. This book is a must for anyone seeking more balance, harmony and joy in their life!"

- Terri Cole, Psychotherapist and
Best-Selling Author of *Boundary Boss*

Siu's unique step-by-step approach to addressing the current mental crisis in our society is a winning formula. Her use of Qigong and Chinese medicine theories to get in touch with our spiritual side is invaluable in maintaining balance in modern societies full of extremes and excesses. Whether you are a novice or a master spiritualist, this book is a must-read for those who seek energetic and spiritual balance in their life.

- Dr. Thomas Leung, CEO Kamwo Meridian Herbs,
Professor at Pacific College of Oriental Medicine

What a pleasure to see how Siu Ping uses Qigong to help and inspire people.

- Master Robert Peng

Similar to Siu, I left an analytical, left-brained, pattern-recognition consulting career to become an alternative medicine practitioner, so I very much appreciate and applaud this compelling read where logic meets the spiritual!

Stronger than Your Stress is more than a stress management book. Bravo to Siu for providing a tangible guide and set of Qigong exercises to check aside our "dominating brain" and to allow us to better connect our mental, emotional and physical dots to our intuitive spirit. I will be recommending Siu's thoughtful book to all my patients so they, too, can overcome and gently release repressed emotional stress, strengthen their spiritual center, and live their healthiest and best selves.

- Dr. Dan Wunderlich, Director of Integrative Acupuncture & Bodywork and Founder of Global Healthworks Foundation, a humanitarian outreach

As a doctor of East Asian medicine, I am impressed with how Siu skillfully uses Qigong and concepts of Chinese medicine to heal herself and empower others. I am excited to see this program enhance the mental, emotional, physical and spiritual well-being of all who are fortunate enough to learn from her.

- Dr. Dody Chang, Doctor of Acupuncture & Chinese Medicine and Founder of Dao Collective

Siu has been a transformational healer for more than 20 years. Now, she is cracking the code on how to step out of stress, anxiety and depression by tapping into your inner spirit. Siu is able to break down spiritual concepts and practices, making them easy to understand and incorporate into our daily lives. Plus, her tutorial videos are available through QR codes in the book, which feels like you're in an online class being guided along. If you're suffering right now, like so many are, don't waste another moment... grab this book.

- Tracey Pontarelli, Wellness Entrepreneur

Stronger than Your Stress

An Energy Guide to Heal From Within©

Siu Ping Negrin, L.Ac.

ISBN-13: 978-1-958848-92-0 hardcover edition
ISBN-13: 978-1-958848-93-7 paperback edition
ISBN-13: 978-1-958848-94-4 e-book edition

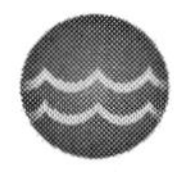

Waterside Productions
2055 Oxford Ave
Cardiff, CA 92007
www.waterside.com

Dedicated to my mom, Yuk Chu Ha,

whose life was sacrificed to bring Heal From Within© to light.

Table of Contents

Introduction

At the age of 38, after enjoying a lifetime of good health, I suffered a sudden, crippling bout of insomnia. This came on the heels of 16 years of the trials and tribulations of life in Manhattan. After only 8 months of marriage, I found myself supporting my husband back to health after a recurrence of his Hodgkin's lymphoma.

A bit later, after he recovered, I underwent 3 grueling years of infertility treatments. During those 3 years, I was also enrolled in a master's program in Chinese medicine and acupuncture, having quit my 12-year-long, lucrative computer consulting business. With the help of Chinese medicine, I was elated to become a mother of two girls. Just as I enthusiastically put up my own shingle to heal the world, my life came to a halt with this sudden loss of sleep.

Not to worry because I had plenty of tools, western and eastern, at my disposal for what I considered a brief bump in the road. All of them provided temporary fixes or minimal improvements, but no significant relief to this health crisis that lasted *nearly 14 years.*

The struggle to return to my formerly healthy and resilient self became increasingly frantic and discouraging. I was forced to explore what most people would consider "conventions beyond my intellect." This led me to understand that the energetic connection to our spirit and universe is an integral part of our health. It was through my personal Tao (path) that I eventually discovered what a soul is, where it lives in me, and most importantly, a tangible way of connecting to it. It was only this knowledge that allowed me to become stronger than my stress and regain wholistic health, peace and happiness.

My name is Siu Ping Negrin, and I'm a Qigong healer, spiritual coach, acupuncturist and lifelong student of Chinese medicine and its philosophy: the root of our existence comes from living in energetic harmony with the universe. The simple Taoist notion of energetic free flow is what led me to the cure that was inside me all along: returning to my soul, the body's spiritual organ.

Whether you are here to find ways to improve your health, take back your life from the madness of stress, enjoy more peace of mind or even find a deeper spiritual connection to yourself, the universe or a higher power, I will show you the path is the same.

I start by asking you to shift your mindset from one of seeking relief and hoping for health, peace and happiness to that of setting a new goal: creating energetic free flow in your life. My promise to you is that if you allow me to tangibly guide this flow back to your soul, you will improve your overall well-being. Flow is the key, no matter what your situation is: sick, stressed, anxious, depressed, feeling stuck, hopeless or helpless. In flow, you will understand that health, peace and happiness are not states that you can consciously acquire but instead come naturally from living in an awakened, soulful state.

Journey Back to Me

From as far back as I can remember, I have always had an inner voice guiding me. This voice calmed me and made me feel safe, loved and empowered to make choices that were aligned with my best interest. Now, whether I listened to it or not was a different matter altogether. But there was comfort in knowing that I had full power to choose how to process and experience the many difficulties life was throwing at me. I knew I could rely on my inner voice, even when the outer world seemed to be failing me over and over again.

Born in 1963, my beginnings in Hong Kong were humble indeed. Yuk Chu Ha, my mom, was pregnant with me (her fifth child) when she suffered a mental breakdown. She would eventually be diagnosed with schizophrenia. My father was the product of the typical patriarchal Asian society, a culture that treated women as second-class citizens and condoned flagrant womanizing, gambling and drinking. I have very little memory of my dad for the first six years of my life. He was mostly absent, working on ships as a cook, traveling and enjoying the life of an "uncommitted man."

You get the picture: a schizophrenic mother raising four kids on her own, with the third daughter dying around the age of 2—from pneumonia, presumably. Fortunately, we did have "Aunt" Goo-paw, who helped raise us. Having our "cousins" nearby was our saving grace. All I knew as a little girl was that Mom was crazy. I heard the whispers: "Will those kids be OK?" "Must be so hard for her husband!" "What's going to happen to all of them?" The scariest of all was, "I think it runs in her family."

My dad came home after an extended absence. It had been so long since we'd seen him that I distinctly remember wondering who this man was. He announced, "We are going to America!" He had gotten sponsors, no easy feat back in 1969, by developing relationships as a chef working on naval ships while traveling around the world.

Off we went to the land of opportunity, landing in Far Rockaway. Within a year, we moved to Manhattan to live in a Lower East Side tenement—a 5-story walk-up. Foreign land, new language and the food—yuck! Living in a small apartment with five children (my younger sister was born in Manhattan) and a desperately sick wife was a real ball and chain for my dad. Our new arrangements didn't give him the autonomy he craved.

A year later, we moved to a house in Levittown, Long Island, the place that would become my home until I graduated college. Dad was soon off working far away from his family, once again enjoying the freedom to gamble, drink and live like a bachelor. He came home every month or so for a weekend.

I can't be sure why my dad chose Levittown. Was it affordable housing, a better life in the suburbs or a place far enough from the Chinese community to allow my father to continue living his untethered life with some discretion? We happened to be flanked by a couple of neighbors who had children with special needs. I heard rumblings that they lived in this neighborhood because there was a good school and resources nearby to support them. Maybe my dad was aware of this and was hoping to help my mom.

I can't be sure how much he knew or how much he tried to help, but it was in Levittown that my mother was officially diagnosed as schizophrenic. On occasions, there were some futile attempts to force-feed her medications, which she generally resisted, leaving her unmedicated until I was an adult.

My home life was truly chaotic. The kids took care of themselves, each other and our mentally ill mom. For most of our life in Levittown, my family had no car, so we walked everywhere. Once every couple of weeks, we would walk the two miles to the supermarket with just enough money left to take a taxi home with all our groceries. For many years, we had no washer and dryer and walked the two miles back and forth to the laundromat, hauling all our clothes.

My mom lived in the past in her own paranoid world. She was constantly screaming throughout the house and our yard in Wenchownese, my parents' native dialect that I had never learned. During severe episodes, she would walk around naked outside. Sometimes she would wander off in the neighborhood. There were also times when she became violent and had to be institutionalized.

My entire life revolved around taking care of the household, going to school, doing homework, and working whatever job I could find from the age of 10. I took over being the head of the household at 13 when my older sister left for work and college. At 16, I started working a lot more after school and on weekends. There was very little joy in my life.

Not to mention that Levittown was an all-white neighborhood, and prejudice was rampant. We were the only non-white family in Levittown in the seventies. You can imagine what it was like for me growing up there: having recently arrived from Hong Kong with the odd name Siu Ping Ha, a schizophrenic mother and absent father ... not a fun time. I was constantly ridiculed for being Chinese, smart, nerdy, awkward-looking and terribly shy.

My family was often the subject of cruel pranks, break-ins and other tormenting exploits. At the age of 14, I was sexually molested. That's what happens in an unsupervised home. After some time had passed, I finally disclosed the incident to a few people. Without a real resolution, I remained quiet and learned to manage the confusion, shame and guilt on my own. I actually rarely ever spoke at all; I was almost a mute until high school. I bought the family's first car at age 17 with a $1,000 loan from my dad, which I promptly paid back with money earned from my jobs.

Owning that car was the beginning of my physical freedom and my finally beginning to speak up a bit. My car gave me the freedom and confidence to express myself outwardly; I was able to meet people outside my lonely and trapped world. I became the first one in my family to go to a four-year university and left for SUNY Albany—paid for through personal money saved, loans and financial aid.

I will end the stories of my early years there—not because there were no other future traumas in my life ... as you know, there were. I struggled to understand how my personal downfall happened nearly twenty years later, when I became a healer, not when I was soldiering through this upbringing. Of course, the more recent years were frantically busy: supporting my husband emotionally and physically, working long hours as a consultant, and studying to become an acupuncturist. Then starting my healing practice and raising two young daughters, all the while trying to maintain my physical health and role as the calm, together supermom, wife and healer.

Despite all the exercise and healthy eating, I was frazzled mentally, emotionally, and, ultimately, physically. During the initial years of insomnia, I explored every western and eastern treatment available to me to no avail. Desperate for relief, I was introduced to Beverly Chapman, an Apache Native American healer, who showed me the power of the spiritual world. Without ever meeting her in person and through only remote healing, she improved my sleep by about 50%. I was so amazed that I decided to do a two-year apprenticeship with her.

Native Americans rely heavily on external spiritual guides to provide answers and healing assistance. There was no denying that her teachings improved my health and boosted my healing powers, which was immediately apparent to my clients. However, my strong sense of self needed to trust something I could control, like the internal voice that had reliably guided me (until recent years, when it fell silent). Without that anchor, I felt stress and intensity creeping back into my life. With this new spiritual world opened to me, I left to seek out other masters to make different connections.

After studying with several, I met Master Robert Peng. He taught me his style of Qigong, which consisted of gentle breathing and movements that balance Qi (energy) in the body. Much to my surprise, within 2 weeks of following his videos, my sleep remarkably returned back to 100%. Once again, I could fall asleep easily and wake feeling refreshed after a full night of peaceful sleep. How could an ailment that I had suffered from for nearly 14 years and that had driven me nearly to madness disappear so suddenly? Something powerful had shifted in me subconsciously.

Instead of getting stuck on trying to understand this miracle on an intellectual level, I simply continued my practice and studies with Master Peng. One of the principles of Chinese medicine is "where there is no free flow, there is pain; where there is free flow, there is no pain." Master Peng's Qigong was able to bring my Qi to a free-flowing state and thus relieve my ailment in a way no other technique—including acupuncture, herbs, other Qigong and spiritual practices—had been able to do. Even beyond my physical body, my personal spiritual center had begun to burgeon.

It was then I strongly reconnected to the internal voice that had faithfully helped me weather all the storms in my earlier life. With little family support and few role models growing up, I had intuitively drawn from this internal source for strength and survival. After returning back to my healthy self, I realized that my insomnia and illness were the results of losing that connection. Without that voice, I did many things that depleted my well-being and did not serve my best interest.

Lacking knowledge of the spirit and soul, I believed that this wisdom lived in my smart brain instead of my soul. As society increasingly focused on the development of the brain, so did my intense reliance on the brain to navigate my life, which led to my uncontrollable stress. I believe the major contributing factor to the stress epidemic today is our lack of connection to the grounding forces of spirit. Without a relationship to our spiritual organ, the Qi in our brains, bodies and hearts is left unanchored, disconnected and misguided.

It's no wonder that all the knowledge in the world couldn't stop me from being overwhelmed with stress and anxiety—or cure my insomnia. I had unknowingly allowed my dominating brain to squash the voice of my soul. Once I understood the dynamic between the two, I could balance their energies and return to living more cohesively. With the powerful language of Qi and Qigong as my cultivation tool, I could now strengthen my relationship with this spiritual organ and de-power the brain's control.

I then felt called to help people live a more fulfilled life, one with less struggle and suffering. I wanted to help them as Master Peng did for me. This urge, along with reading the life-changing *Inner Engineering: A Yogi's Guide To Joy* by Sadhguru, inspired the birth of the Heal From Within© 9-week program. Many of my clients joined this program seeking relief from unrelenting stress, anxiety, fears, or depression. Many more also had physical ailments such as gastrointestinal pain, insomnia, chronic pain and even cancer. They all felt that their issues were exacerbated by their compromised mental and emotional health.

Others came seeking more meaning, fulfillment and spirituality in their lives. What nearly every one of my clients has in common is that they searched for years (like me), trying many techniques—yoga, mindfulness, various meditations, other Qigong styles, apps, retreats and therapies—looking for an answer. Some have also been left feeling hopeless after going from doctor to doctor, getting batteries of tests and trying many medications that left them with side effects and minimal relief.

Seeing one client after another succeed with the program gave me the confidence to offer a 100% happiness guarantee if they weren't satisfied after completion. As of the writing of this book, I have not given any refund to a graduate. I knew I had something big to share with the world, which led me to write this book. I want to get this simple, doable and effective program out to the widest possible audience. May the knowledge in these pages help you find whatever it is that you are seeking.

I am honored to be the Heal From Within© guide to strengthen your energetic connection to the universe.

夏少萍 Ha Siu Ping

Personal Goals

I have found it helpful when beginning any new endeavor to think ahead to the desired end result. I would like you to write down on the lines below the goals you would like to achieve by the end of this program.

Think big, think broad! Here are some of the most common goals I see in my practice: to create more space in my mind; to remove painful memories of my past, so they don't affect me now; to feel better physically; to have less pain; to sleep better; to move on more easily from things I have outgrown or lost (jobs, relationships, friendships, etc.); to stop beating myself up all the time and become more confident in my decision-making; to be a good role model for my children (this is probably the most common desire I see from parents); to love myself more; and to be able to keep the stress out of my body so I can stay healthy.

Guess what… this is all possible. What do you want to achieve?

Let's meet a few of my clients and hear why they chose to join HFW©:

1. Ann Graziosi was a retired microbiologist and a single mother of 2 girls, both of whom were struggling with serious health issues. During COVID, the

exhaustion finally caught up with her leaving her tank empty – 4:23 min.

2. Suzy was going through a difficult time raising her teenage son and dealing with a divorce. Being a spiritual person, she wanted to improve her intuition to help her through this challenging time – 1:51 min.

3. Molly Bacon, an elementary school teacher and yoga instructor, found that her relationships with her children, husband and other members of her family were not what they once were. She was becoming short-tempered, and she knew something needed to change – 2:41 min.

My goal(s)—what I'd like to achieve with Heal From Within©:

____

____

____

____

____

____

____

____

____

____

Heal From Within© Theory

A mathematician at heart, I seek tried and true formulas to live by. In my opinion, formulas provide assurance that is hard to beat because following them will produce the same result each time. Moreover, math is like life; the more we learn, the more equations we will discover.

Heal From Within© is predicated on the simple Taoist theory that all living organisms in the universe are energetically connected. Humans, animals and plants are born from the earth and absorb energy from the same sources—sun, water and air—for survival. Living congruently to this energy flow allows you to vibrate at your highest frequency and better manage life's afflictions, such as viruses, disease, trauma, stress). The less resistance in your body, the easier it is to attain your maximum personal healing potential and live in a healthier and more fulfilling way. Learning how to apply this Taoist theory to your life will help you live at your highest frequency under all circumstances.

The Formula

Heal From Within© is my humble attempt to show you how to live in alignment with the universe. This process will help you overcome your challenges and lead you to the beacon of your wisdom. The formula is composed of 3 concurrent processes of energetic balancing—Release, Restore, Return—aka the 3Rs.

1. First: RELEASE. Release the energetic charge stuck in your body that is the result of negativity from your thoughts, emotions, traumas from the past, fears and anxieties in the present, or worry about the future.
2. Second: RESTORE. Once the negative energy transforms or loosens, restore your body by bringing in positive Qi to reorganize and rebalance the flow, thereby recharging you.
3. Finally: RETURN. A return to your inner self. By releasing and restoring, you'll uncover the YOU that is there somewhere deep inside. You will hear your inner voice, feel safe, see your internal light and rediscover the wonderful undamaged original you. You can know yourself, love yourself and get back in touch with your soul.

All three parts are done concurrently, not in phases. The need to continually release, restore and return is ongoing. You will always face new and different challenges in your daily life; the goal is to stay ahead of them. Note I said, "Stay ahead," not just manage symptoms. You need to become strong enough to prevent stress, anxiety, depression and their debilitating effects from weakening you and taking up residence in your body and life.

You can become stronger than your stress.

Just like all mathematical formulas, the validity of the 3Rs comes from its ability to produce the same results under all circumstances. So I invite you to learn the HFW© formula, practice it, and apply it to your daily life. It will bring you to a better state of being, as certain as 2+2 = 4.

Let this formula bring free-flowing energy to your inner self to improve every facet of your life: mental clarity, emotional calm, physical health, and spiritual connection.

How to Succeed with This Program

This program is unique in that it provides a simple step-by-step formula of tangible energetic tools to help you make long-lasting inner transformations. To achieve that, it is not sufficient to teach you how to manage your stress; you must learn how *to keep the stress outside of you as much as possible.* Of course, none of us can avoid fender-benders, tough days at work, breakups, arguments with a friend, too much to do…and the hundred and one other things that stress us out. However, if you follow this formula, stress and its damaging effects on your health and well-being will no longer take root deep inside of you, allowing for much greater peace of mind, resilience and flow to your spirit.

If you would like to have similar successes to my other clients, I suggest you approach this book in one of two ways: 1) Model my online program by reading one chapter a week along with practicing the accompanying Qigong exercises. 2) Read the entire book first to become familiarized with the teachings and then return to learning one chapter a week while practicing Qigong.

Heal From Within© may present many ideas that are new to you. The work is comprehensive and unblocks your constrained energy layer by layer in the process of making you whole. Each person is unique and will experience "aha" moments at varying points of the online process, which usually happens somewhere between chapters 2–6. As you read the book, remain open-minded, and as your energy transforms, you can expect to have a similar experience. The exercises are extremely simple, gentle and pleasant and accessed via QR codes throughout each chapter. This program is safe for people of all ages and physical abilities.

HFW© is about recalibrating your Qi on a comprehensive, wholistic level. This can only be done by understanding its philosophy along with practicing the corresponding Qigong exercises. Reading about them without putting the exercises into practice will only temporarily shift your mindset and provide momentary relief. The many new concepts you learn will only come alive with the continuous cultivation of Qi.

Let's hear how Jonathan, a Chinese educator with a strong understanding of Chinese philosophy, realized that he couldn't succeed without putting what he knew into practice - 1:27 min.

Over the weeks, as you gradually feel better, at first, like me, you may not even understand why. Along the way, more connections will be made. My suggestion is to put all analysis aside and just experience. Let this journey lead you to free flow, and the truth will be revealed over time.

These teachings and techniques are based on my interpretations of the laws of nature and the universe. They are drawn from my Chinese medicine studies, innate beliefs and what was shown to me through my Qigong meditations. Like Chinese medicine, these insights are then applied to all aspects of life: food, medicine, exercise, cognition and lifestyle. Since we are born from the universe, it only makes sense that what works for the mother will also work for its child.

How can you maximize your success on this energy journey?

·Approach this program with a "beginner's mind," meaning put aside whatever preconceived ideas you may have from experience or previous teachings. Do not let those ideas impede your new learning. There will be many concepts that are probably new to you throughout this book; some readers will take to them quickly. For others, it will take some time for the brain to allow these new ideas in. I will not ask you to have faith. Instead, I ask you to test out the process and see how it works out for you.

·Make the commitment. You are not committing to me, Chinese medicine principles or even the idea of Qi. You are committing to healing yourself with some of these tried-and-true principles. There are 9 Heal From Within© Qigong exercises and meditations, each under 10 minutes, associated with each step of the program. All are powerful and, over time, will help to immediately center, ground and fill you with positive Qi. With these energy cultivation practices, your Qi will accumulate, and you will feel substantial benefits in your body and life.

When I first developed this program, I realized my shortfall was not being able to provide the proper support for my clients. COVID-19 forced me, along with most of the world, to go virtual. This silver lining allowed me to bring the program online and provide regular live support to help my clients achieve maximum success. I encourage you to join me live so I can do the same for you.

·Follow this guide patiently and practice it in the way it was developed. As an acupuncture student, I needled the same way my teacher did; when I studied Qigong, I practiced like my master. I gave it my all, and as I allowed the teachings to become woven into my being, I defined a style that was uniquely mine.

My program is like most therapies, including acupuncture. You can't determine the program's effectiveness unless you give it the necessary time. That doesn't mean you must wait until the end for results. At the end of each chapter, you will find codes for resetting your mind. As you do the Qigong exercises and these codes are downloaded into your cellular memory, you will feel better and better as you become more whole, chapter by chapter.

Fundamental Program Principles

Balance of Yin and Yang

Balance is a fundamental philosophy in Chinese medicine for life and well-being. In Chinese philosophy, yin and yang are two opposing forces that complement each other and together create a perfect balance. Yin symbolizes feminine energy, nighttime, nourishment and rest; Yang symbolizes masculine energy, daytime, vibrancy and activity. Neither aspect is superior, and one naturally feeds into and supports the other. The Yin-Yang symbol perfectly represents the dynamic motion of these opposing forces in creating a unity of the whole.

The human body is an amazing machine. We have built-in Yin-Yang mechanisms in place to keep us in homeostasis. Whenever we are sick or stressed, the body's immune system activates, then self-regulates to bring us back into balance when the crisis is over.

In a distressing situation, the body's sympathetic nervous system uses all its energy to prepare to fight or flee the perceived danger. The heartbeat and breath rate accelerates to provide energy and oxygen as the muscles tense up for strength. Whatever is not needed for immediate survival is put on the back burner. Meaning:

digestion, reproductive and growth hormone production and tissue repair are all temporarily suspended. When the stressful event is over, the Yin parasympathetic takes over again, the body relaxes, and energy returns to all parts of the body. This happens naturally without any conscious thought.

Unfortunately, our rushed modern lifestyle tends to keep our bodies in a heightened state of fight-or-flight, meaning we can get stuck in a prolonged Yang sympathetic state of imbalance. Prolonged stress can create stress wounds; wounds leave scars in the body (similar to scarring from surgery, which can cause adhesions, pain, disfigurement and restrict mobility). "Stress scars" can also compromise the body permanently and are to be avoided at all costs. This is why my approach is to keep you as strong as possible from the inside out, so your body's natural response can successfully defend itself from stress and quickly restore optimum balance.

Free Flow

A free flow state is where we thrive by operating at maximum power using minimal effort. Just watch people who are highly accomplished in their particular field—from actors and musicians to athletes. One thing they all have in common is they make difficult tasks seem effortless. Tennis great Roger Federer looks like he's barely breaking a sweat when he plays a four-hour match. Or watch a gazelle run—it almost looks like it is gliding across the land. Elite athlete or animal: the entire system is perfectly in sync, like a well-tuned machine, which allows them to accomplish the task with more ease.

The more you learn to create and maintain free flow, the sooner you will manage daily responsibilities and tasks with more ease—and experience far more enjoyment while doing them.

Let's hear Molly describe what freer energy flow feels like - 12 sec.

Qi

In the West, we think of Qi as simply energy, but the Chinese consider it a vital life force that powers all action. Qi is the energetic force that materializes to transform your intents, thoughts and emotions into reality. When you think dark thoughts or feel down or depressed, this negative energy vibrates at a lower frequency and passes through your body as a heavy, constricting feeling. Of course, the opposite is also true: when you feel happy, your whole body flows freely, feels light and sings. Positive energy transforms quickly in your body, whereas negative energy remains in your system longer and is more difficult to clear. These energies create a negative or positive physical reality in your body and life.

To further complicate matters, the brain is prone to keeping negative thoughts and emotions stuck inside of us, trapping us in an endless loop. Science has shown that repeated experiences can alter the neural pathways in the brain, which then influence how a person experiences the world. Their past experiences cause them to respond through a lens of strength, fear, happiness or trauma. The earlier we can transform any negative energy, the less opportunity it has to block flow and form negative neural pathways.

All energy can be shifted with the right techniques.

By learning how to transform the flow of your own thoughts and emotions, you can live in control and become stronger than your stress.

Qigong: The Practice of Cultivating Qi

The principal source of Qi comes from food and the cosmos: air, sun, water and the moon. We use energy from our environment to nourish our bodies. When you connect to the Qi in your body, you are connecting to this external universal energy source. This is why living in harmony with the world is so important to your livelihood.

The Chinese recognized the importance of Qi and developed an entire medical system to learn how to cultivate it. Chinese medicine is basically energy medicine—it's all about keeping your life force strong and flowing. *Gong* means practice—so Qigong is the practice of cultivating your internal life force fueled by the universe.

As Qi travels through your body via pathways called meridians, it transforms into different forms of usable energy. For example, as the Air Qi moves through your body, it gets processed into Lung Qi to help you breathe, Stomach Qi for digestion, and so on, to support all your bodily functions. In the West, we would define these various energy forms in the body as mechanical assistance to help you move, electrical stimulation for your heart and brain, and thermal regulation of your body temperature.

We use generators and panels to capture renewable energy sources (sun, wind, water) to power our busy lives. Can our bodies also absorb energy like this? Of course, we are living energy panels! We wouldn't be alive if we couldn't convert the sun's rays and oxygen from the air and water into energy that our bodies can use.

The Chinese understood that and developed over generations a system of Qigong exercises that allows you to maximize this energetic charge. Think of these practices as plugging into the power source of Universal Qi—the same way your cell phone plugs into a socket to be charged.

Creating usable energy always requires some form of motion. To create nuclear energy, we split an atom; to create thermal energy, we rub two pieces of wood together. What activity converts the energy around you into something usable for your body?

It all begins with breathing. It may seem too simplistic and obvious that it could be that easy, but it is. And by adding gentle flowing movements, we will enhance the flow of Qi throughout the body. This is the first building block of the program.

Qi Breath - The Building Block to Heal From Within©

Qi Breath is the basis of Heal From Within© Qigong. It is also the opposite of the kind of breathing most of us have been accustomed to doing, so it may take some time to get used to.

Qi Breath is gentle, slow and long. As you bring the breath in through your nose, your body contracts and concentrates the energy. When you exhale, most of the air flows throughout your body, creating a nice, relaxing, floating feeling. Your body will naturally expel the air it doesn't need out of your mouth and pores—without any conscious effort on your part.

This exercise is hard for many people at the beginning because of all the different styles of breathing people have become accustomed to, for example, yoga, abdominal and mindful. Some people have developed the habit of breathing only through the nose or mouth. It is important to master Qi Breath because this is the basic breath we will use in all the exercises you will learn going forward.

Qigong's benefits can only be cultivated through practice, and the breath is where it begins. Qi is real because air is real. When you breathe in oxygen, it gives you life. If you allow your body to relax and let the Qi flow through your gentle breath, you maximize the absorption of the air's healing properties. It may take some time to develop the sensitivity to feel the Qi moving through your body, but each Qigong exercise will bring you one step closer.

Until you feel the Qi, don't overthink it during your practice. The more relaxed and less focused you are and intent upon results, the faster it will just happen—naturally. Just let this breath in. The body processes your respiration without any mental control; you only need to get out of its way to receive its maximum benefit.

Your energy shifts with each Qi breath, and from week to week, your Qi will flow more freely. How will you know that it's working? Your body will start to feel better, whether you feel the Qi or not.

Let's practice Qi breath together - 7:11 min.

If you have difficulty with this breath, first practice inhaling through the nose and exhaling out the mouth. Then practice contracting your body inward as you inhale, then relaxing, opening and filling your body during the exhale. Master this breath, and you will be able to feel an energy shift pretty quickly every time you do the Heal From Within© Qigong exercises.

Let's hear Ann talk about her struggles with Qi Breath and how she overcame them to change her life - 4:28 min.

Free Flow Breathing meditation is a great way to practice your Qi Breath and get your Qi flowing into the ultimate relaxation.

Let's soothe our Qi with Free Flow Breathing meditation - 10 min.

The Intelligence of Qi

Master Peng taught me that "Qi is smarter than us." I must admit that it took me some time to believe and trust this statement. However, the more I worked with Qi and learned not to fight it, the more I came to realize this truth.

Every living organism knows how to absorb the healing power of the water, air and sun without any thought, analysis or effort. Heal From Within© is essentially a guide to help you get out of your own way to let this healing process occur as naturally and efficiently as possible. As sure as the sun creates vitamin D in the body without you even being aware of it, the intelligence of Qi can release blockages, restore free flow and return you back to your inner light, truth and strength. Just allow.

Chapter 1 - Balancing the 4 Energy Centers

Reminders:

- *Practice Qi Breath as much as you can at any time of the day. This daily Qigong will set the foundation for the rest of the exercises in this program.*
- *You can practice Qi Breath anywhere… just do it for a few minutes at a time, and soon enough, breathing deeply and calmly will become your immediate meditative tool for stress relief.*

The 4 Main Energy Centers

Chinese medicine (CM) takes a wholistic view of the body, one that is comprised of both physical and non-physical substances (Qi and spirit, rather than blood or bones, for example). In contrast to Western medicine, CM emphasizes the health of both the anatomical structure and its own unique system of non-physical attributes. Thus, energy centers are a non-physical concept found in Eastern studies but not in the West.

Those of you who have studied yoga may be familiar with the chakras, a Sanskrit word that originated in India. Practitioners believe there are 7 main energy centers in the body, starting with the root chakra at the base of the spine and ascending to the crown chakra at the top of the head.

In Chinese medicine meditative and exercise practice, there are 3 focal energy centers, known as dantians, in the body—Upper (wisdom), Middle (love) and Lower (vitality). The dantians are known as a "sea of qi" or "elixir field" where the Qi in our bodies is concentrated. The three dantians store and control Qi and Qi's potential.

Master Peng's Qigong also emphasizes the Central Meridian, the energy channel that connects all 3 dantians to the universe. Activating and keeping the 3 energy centers and central channel balanced and strong is the basis of all Master Peng's and HFW©'s Qigong practices.

The Upper Dantian is the energy center that houses the brain and all its functions, including the third eye, which in Eastern medicine is used to perceive beyond what's visible and expand one's wisdom. The entry point to this center is located in between the eyebrows at the level of your third eye. A strong Upper Dantian allows you to have sharp perception, awareness, and understanding beyond what is known to us.

The Middle Dantian is located in your chest and houses your heart and emotional energy, along with the Eastern concepts of spiritual and mental consciousness which will be explained later in this chapter. The entry point to this center is located in between your breasts on the sternum, level with your nipples. Keeping the energy flowing is critical in keeping your heart calm and opening the gateway to your soul.

The Lower Dantian is located in your lower abdomen and houses your digestive and reproductive organs. It is responsible for creating your physical form and supporting your vitality. In the Chinese medicine construct, it is linked to your inherited prenatal essence, which is considered the DNA in the West and provides you with a lifetime energy reserve. The entry point to this center is located a couple of inches below the navel. Preservation of this energy determines the quality and longevity of your physical health and gives you the strength you need to manifest your destiny.

The Central Meridian is a channel that runs through the center of your body. It extends upward above the crown of your head, connecting to the sky, and downward below your perineum, connecting to the depths of the earth. Having a strong Central Meridian ensures a clear roadway that allows your 3 dantians to flow freely and align with the universe. If the central meridian is blocked, we become disconnected. Your brain, heart and body will not communicate well with each other as each energy center acts on its own behalf. When we operate in this asynchronous manner, it's as if we are playing disjointed instruments in a bad orchestra.

Having integrated the Chinese medicine concept of energy centers with the Western paradigm of science, I offer another higher-level view of our being: one where the body has 4 main energy centers. I have termed the centers as **mental, emotional, physical and spiritual** and believe that optimal wholistic health comes from keeping all four strong.

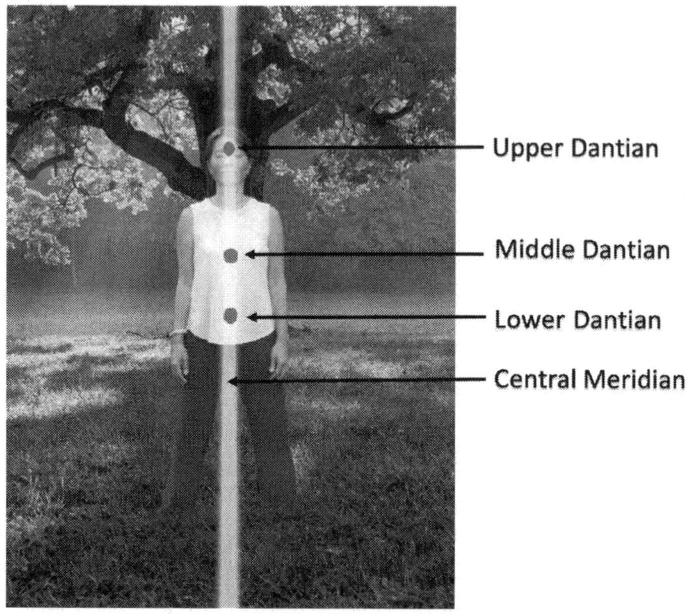

Strength and good health can only be achieved when all 4 centers are flowing freely and coordinated with each other. Just as in any well-run family or corporation: when the components work together, there will be less conflict and greater organization, enjoyment and productivity.

If one energy center takes over, then the other centers cannot be in sync, compromising your balance, free flow and overall health.

The Dictator Brain

Western and Chinese medicines have vastly different concepts of the brain. In the West, the brain is a complex organ that controls every process that regulates your body: motor control, thought, memory, emotion, and the 5 senses. This is certainly a lot of power for one organ. This is unlike Chinese medicine, where the brain is considered an "extraordinary" organ, with all its functions dispersed among the other organs in the body. Specifically, the consciousness of the mind resides in the heart and not the brain. With these various functions spread throughout the body, the brain is thus dependent on the health of all the organs and the entire body.

It is my belief that the root cause of stress today is our Western notion of the brain, which has created what I call the Dictator Brain.

Western culture places a high premium on intelligence and remaining "sharp" throughout our lives. Our emphasis on mental development has created the all-powerful brain, which now truly believes it is the greatest and in charge. Unfortunately, we are paying the price because this all-powerful organ has now become a dictator. We live in a paradox: promoting this dictator yet trying desperately to overcome the trap of our own thoughts to relieve stress, anxiety and depression—to name just a few common maladies of modern life.

Current therapies addressing mental and emotional health have not been notably successful. The objective of cognitive behavior therapy (CBT) is to retrain thought and behavioral patterns. These are deeply ingrained and hard to alter because the habits of your brain are so strongly reinforced by social, familial and educational influences. Change requires diligence, willpower and mental energy; none of which are easily available when stressed. This is why it is hard to sustain the lessons of CBT in the long run.

Another common form of therapy is psychoanalysis, where, in sessions with a trained therapist, unconscious conflicts are examined as they are presumed to be much of the reason for the patient's behavior. Through understanding these often deeply repressed conflicts, the hope is that the behavior will change. Unfortunately, reasoning doesn't work with a dictator. Once the brain has become a dictator, its only goal is to remain in power. The brain does not care about the whys of the past; it vigilantly tells you what to do, relentlessly, today and every day.

We are literally not in control of our own minds anymore; instead, they control us. The brain simply doesn't listen when we plead with or order ourselves to relax or keep things in perspective; our thoughts increasingly spin out of control. In order to take back some of the control the brain has over us, we need to reduce its dominance, which is exactly what this program will set out to help you do.

The Mental Center

You have learned the importance of keeping Qi flowing freely and have started to practice attaining it with a simple Qi Breath. However, what you now need is to be aware of what *impedes* the flow of Qi. Once you've brought in good Qi with your breathing, it would be a waste not to maintain it.

In order to restore free flow, you need to understand how you can maximize your flow by minimizing the personal tension that blocks it. Is your stress caused by physical injury, overwork or poor diet? Or grief or traumas that have left emotional scars that have never been resolved, or even thoughts that are incongruent with your spiritual sensibility? All these can and do ultimately affect your body's energy flow because strife manifests as blockages in the body.

Chinese medicine practitioners heal illnesses by examining their patients' signs and symptoms and identifying the disharmonious pattern in the person's body that has caused this energetic disruption. We then provide our clients with insight into how they might correct these patterns so they can maintain their own well-being. When the cause is from a physical injury or diet, it is seemingly easier to correct. But when the cause is emotional or mental in nature, it is made much more difficult when the dictator brain is causing the problem.

Many of us walk around, never realizing that the things we say, think or do have a significant impact on our health. I have mentioned how your thoughts and emotions can contribute to either a positive or blocked flow. Blocked flow creates distress in the body and, unless it is cleared, will accumulate. This can contribute over time to ailments such as anxiety, stress, depression, aches, pains, insomnia, autoimmune disease and even cancer. My aim is to tangibly demonstrate how these negative moments can impact your health—and, more importantly, how you have the power to transform them.

Good thoughts and feelings create free flow and good health. Negative thoughts and feelings create blockages that inhibit your well-being.

As we discussed, dictators do not willingly cede control. Therefore, in order to eliminate the dictator brain's negative influence on your mind, you must harness the power of your other energy centers. Just as in war, you need help from your allies to take control back. In other words, you need help from your other energy centers—the Emotional, Physical and Spiritual.

The Emotional Center

In CM, the emotions are connected to the organs outside the brain. Those connections are: Heart-joy, Lung-grief, Liver-anger, Spleen-worry and Kidney-fear. Thus, the brain's conscious function and the emotion of joy both reside in the heart.

It's interesting to note that in both Chinese and Western medicine, despite their different anatomical and energetic theories, the mind is directly affected by emotions. According to the Chinese, anxiety and depression are a matter of the spirit of the mind which is adversely affected by the lack of joy (sadness), with both aspects residing in the heart. This explains why emotions have such a strong impact on the mind's judgment. A disturbed mind is caused by errant emotions left unchecked.

Since emotions are a distinct group of feelings that all affect mental health, I felt it was appropriate to classify them into one energetic center called the Emotional Center, irrespective of where they reside. A strong emotional center is one that is calm all around. When our emotions are heightened, whether it be anger, grief, anxiety, fear or even great joy, we become highly reactive and do not think clearly. We misjudge and overreact. Such high emotions create frenetic and negative energy. If we leave these toxic emotions unresolved and repressed, they will brew stress, anxiety and/or depression.

However, emotions must not be controlled. They are natural expressions of your state of mind—or, according to the Chinese, the organs which feed the mind. It is only when the emotions become extreme or uncontrolled that they cause health problems, including a disturbed mental state. To return your mind to a calm and healthy place, you must clear the emotional charge instead of trying to control your emotions.

During my studies, I often wondered how my mom's schizophrenia could be the result of a disturbed heart, according to Chinese medicine theory. In an attempt to understand my mom's illness, I surprisingly found a Chinese psychologist, a field that didn't exist in the Asian community back in the '90s. The doctor questioned my mom's schizophrenic diagnosis, given the late onset of her symptoms at the age of 32. She believed my mom may have suffered from postpartum depression that was left untreated after the birth of my older brother.

Still, the questions remain ... whether the "official" diagnosis is schizophrenia, postpartum depression or any other mental health malady, can we treat the disturbed mind and spirit of the heart? How can Chinese medicine, in all its wisdom, not have a way to help patients with these mental and emotional conditions?

Unfortunately, in my mother's case, we will never know. Nonetheless, since she displayed schizophrenic symptoms, the treatment plan at the time was the right course of action. Still, this new theory left me with even more questions. Of course, postpartum depression has a strong hormonal component, but is it possible that the hormones exacerbated an energy blockage or a negative neural pathway that existed before the pregnancy? If so, mustn't we also address the causes of these repeated negative patterns of thought or emotion?

As in everything, start with the basics when searching for answers. In Chinese medicine, we go to its Taoist text, *Tao te Ching*, a book of 81 poems written by philosopher and scholar Lao-Tzu. *Tao* means Path or Way, *te* means virtue or divine, and *Ching* means classics, so the title translates as "The Book of the Path to a Divine Life." It combines metaphors of nature and Taoist wisdom to guide us to live a life of virtue and excellence. Once again, if we abide by the lessons from nature, it will help us live a more connected life with less emotional and mental conflict.

Let's take a look at a verse from Chapter 78 of the *Tao te Ching*, "Nothing in the world is as soft and yielding as water. Yet for dissolving the hard and inflexible, nothing can surpass it. The soft overcomes the hard; the gentle overcomes the rigid. Everyone knows this is true, but few can put it into practice. Therefore the Master remains serene in the midst of sorrow. Evil cannot enter his heart." (translation by Stephen Mitchell, 1995)

You, too, can learn to be as yielding and adaptable as water, dissolving anything harmful that might enter your body. Then nothing can break you, and sadness will be diffused before it can enter the heart to disturb the mind.

HFW© hopes you will allow nature's bountiful metaphors and energy to guide you to build a strong emotional center. To assist this process, in Chapter 2 you will learn techniques to transform your displaced negative emotional energy, so your still heart and clear mind can see these lessons from nature more easily. But for the moment, let's continue with your other two allies.

The Physical Center

Our culture today places tremendous emphasis on our physical health because it is the most external and visible part of our being. But you need to remember that your body is just a vessel, and the most important thing is the essence that it holds. This is yet another metaphor that can be found in Chapter 11 of the *Tao te Ching*.

The most important part of any house is those that live inside it.

Certainly it is important to take good care of your vessel, which is the outer shell that protects you. But, in current society, it is trumping the health of your other 3 energy centers.

The body manifests the health of your collective being. It gives you timely, accurate information on how you are experiencing and processing life. Even if your mind chooses to ignore or repress certain events, they will play out in the body at some point. Your body will always show you when you feel good or when something is wrong and needs attention. Pain is an excellent indicator because, without this warning sign, you would live in ignorance and potentially do destructive things to yourself.

Remember, "Where there is pain, there is no free flow." However, instead of figuring out why free flow is blocked, we here in Western society tend to rely on numerous drugs that numb or mitigate the pain, so we can ignore it and keep going.

For mental and emotional health, we have all kinds of drugs to alter chemicals and hormones that make people feel better *despite* their blockages. These drugs serve a purpose, but unfortunately, their use continues to rise and is now trickling down to the younger generation. Since there doesn't seem to be a better alternative and people are left feeling helpless after trying so many things that don't work, reliance on these drugs persists; even though there has recently been a real backlash after a landmark 2022 study concluded that *antidepressants are not associated with improved quality of life in the long run.*

When we suppress or numb our physical symptoms, we can no longer hear the body's warning signs. Medications are a necessary and important part of our healthcare system. But our reliance on drugs that only mitigate symptoms is perpetuating a healthcare system of increasing drug dependence without curing the root cause of our illnesses.

Let's hear how HFW© has helped Ann avoid being affected by the mental illness that has plagued her family - 3:46 min.

I am going to teach you how to listen to your body for both negative and positive responses to help guide you in life.

Abraham Lincoln lived by this principle: "When I do good, I feel good. When I do bad, I feel bad. That's my religion." When something is right, you'll feel as if all the gears are engaged and everything is working together. You will possess an all-knowing feeling of certainty. On the other hand, if something feels wrong—out of sync or not quite right—your body will send out feelings of unease and discomfort. By tuning into these signals, you can use your body as a compass to guide your decision-making.

You will learn how to change the focus from perpetually finding ways to make the body feel good or less bad to viewing pain or discomfort as a barometer, so you can understand what's going on inside. We want to correct the root of the problem so your whole being is balanced and feels good. This is vastly preferable to treating just the physical while the mind and heart still suffer.

To start listening to your body, you must remove the impediment of your dictator brain. You don't want to keep empowering the dominating brain that interferes with the communications from your other centers. To do this, you must be able to give the brain periods of rest and be open to heed the guidance from your other 3 energy centers.

All I ask is that while reading this book and doing the Qigong practices, you check your dominating brain in a separate room, just like you check your coat when you go inside a restaurant—because you don't need it. I understand this may seem a daunting, if not impossible, task. As you progress in the practice, turning off the brain will become easier. The intelligence of Qi will integrate your energy centers and depower the dominant brain. Until this process happens naturally, create the habit of setting the initial intention by telling your brain to take a back seat during the training periods and to listen to the rest of you—your body, emotions and spirit.

Your brain could do with a bit of rest! Do not worry; after your practice, your brain can't help but automatically resume full control. That is until your energy centers can operate more synergistically.

During your breathwork and Qigong, you will start to pay attention to your 5 senses. Just be aware of what you hear, see, feel, taste and smell. All these senses are innate, so you don't need the brain to interpret and interfere with their signals. Over time, you will come to trust these senses as much as you do your thoughts and emotions, just like animals can sense when prey or bad weather is approaching or food and mating are close by.

Stay open to your body's communication. When something feels imbalanced or distressed in the body, know that something has disrupted your free flow. Being aware of these sensations and then pausing to understand and address the cause of the disharmony will help you to be in control of your life.

The Spiritual Center

In Chinese medicine, the Spirit (Shen) is considered a vital substance. Along with Qi (energy), Blood, and Essence (like genetics or DNA), Spirit completes the fabric of our physiological makeup and life. Furthermore, the Central Spirit has 5 branch spirits—Shen, Hun, Po, Yi, and Zhi—that reside in the Heart, Liver, Lungs, Spleen and Kidneys, respectively. I think of them as 5 facets or characteristics (awareness, searching, instinctual, intention and willpower) that make up the collective soul.

I have categorized the collective soul and its branches to operate within the Spiritual Center, similar to how all the different meridians throughout your body operate within a network. In HFW©, we will focus on connecting to the collective soul in the Spiritual Center.

This Spiritual Center is the least understood and most underutilized of the 4 energy centers. The mystery of this center is due to the fact that most of us can't connect to any of its tangible physical aspects. However, I had experienced years of intuitive communication before I realized that it was coming from my soul. I believe this may be true for many of us.

Over time, the location of the soul was revealed to me: deep in the sternum of the Middle Dantian, right behind one of my favorite acupuncture points, CV17. It perplexed me that the soul would reside behind a point simply known as the Chest Center until I learned that this point is also known as "The Source" and "Original Child." In Taoism, these terms represent both the Tao, which is the source of all things, as well as its offspring, the infinite possibilities and potential of the Tao. The soul is the life source, connected to the ultimate source—the universe (or Tao) and leads you to live out your potential.

Learning the soul's identity and location led me to a deeper and more impactful relationship with my soul that continues to improve my life. As in any relationship, it must be continuously nurtured. I have spoken to many people about the location of the soul. Most people believe it lives in the heart, and some have said it lives in the sternum or brain. Others have said they believe it lives in the stomach. However, I believe they are confused by the warning sign that causes discomfort in their stomach after receiving an intuitive communication.

Wherever your soul may live in your body, I encourage you to have patience and understand that the reality of the soul will take some time to be revealed to you. Until you gain this clarity, just continue to follow HFW©, which will lead you to your soul when you are open and ready to acknowledge it. My hope is to make the Spiritual Center as concrete and real as the other 3 and for you to recognize that until now, you have been living your life 3/4 staffed.

To understand what I mean by that, let's compare a 4-cylinder car to your body. What if you only used 3 of the 4 cylinders to drive? One has all the power (mental), one is highly reactive to every bump on the road (emotional), and one you pay the most attention to because it's the most visible (physical). The last (spiritual) you don't even know how to use. Operating on 3 cylinders doesn't allow your car or body to run optimally, certainly not to its fullest capacity. Similarly, with your spiritual center left idle, the other 3 energy centers are simply overworked. People are burning out because they are overloaded, while the spirit is neglected.

As I mentioned above, many have a hard time with the notion of the spirit because they don't know how to reliably access it. Without material proof, it's understandable why. Also, many people tend to associate spirituality with religion. Given all the religious unrest around the world, it is apparent that religion has not helped us live more spiritually. If it had, we would be living peacefully with theological unity or at least mutual tolerance.

While religion and spirituality do have a connection, they can be independent of each other. Spirituality is the non-material essence that resides within an individual and connects them to the life force, G-d or higher power of the universe; it allows them to live from a place of universal love, beauty and kindness. Religion is just one of many vehicles to help you find a spiritual connection.

The only way you can be guided by spirit is to trust it as much as you trust the other 3 centers. You must make "spirit" tangible so you can access it at will. Without the ability to rely on and operate from spirit, you *cannot* successfully take away your brain's dominance.

Life will certainly be much easier if you use every part of your body that you have been blessed with. Learning how to activate the fourth center, the spiritual, will allow you to spread out the workload, work more efficiently and keep you grounded and balanced. Let's off-load some work from the brain, body and heart to your spirit to share some of the burdens.

Let's hear how Jonathan found his sweet spot from being in alignment with all 4 of his energy centers - 2:40 min.

Finger Exercise

Let's do a simple exercise to show you just how strongly the powerful mind can affect your physical body – 1:58 min.

Where your mind goes, your energy follows. This is the basis of positive thinking. Can you imagine what you might accomplish if you could direct your energies like this all the time?

However, maintaining this positive thinking requires a lot of conscious effort; even more so when fighting against your negatively-biased brain that is constantly driving us. Too often, the dictator brain is punitive, critical and pushes you to the brink of exhaustion. This is why I never tell you to think positively—because it's taxing and unsustainable in the long term.

And we know the dictator doesn't like to listen, so instead of fighting with it, you must influence it another way. You will instead empower the other 3 energy centers by keeping Qi flowing freely through them. Being properly nourished, they can rein in, ground, soften and guide the brain to be a team player.

Now let's start to put Qi to work with a few simple routines. This is the beginning—not of more "positive thinking," but of creating positive energy around you.

Personal Space Opening

This simple routine is the beginning of being in charge of your personal energy.

First, you create your personal energy field (or an energy bubble, as my daughter calls it). It is important to have a strong field of protection around you at all times as the first line of defense to prevent negative stress and energy from entering.

Second, you harmonize your energy to be in flow with the universe.

Let's hear how powerful the Personal Space Opening is and watch how it is done - 2:44 min.

I do this routine every day at least once a day, especially before I start my Qigong. You may also find it helpful to use this when you feel uneasy going into a room or space.

If you feel weird doing it in public or in front of people, go to a private space, like a bathroom, and picture yourself in the room while doing this routine.

I have had clients tell me that they have done this exercise when tensions are running high. They get everyone in the room to participate, and it quickly and noticeably changes the atmosphere and energy. If you don't have cooperative people who are willing to join in, surround the people who are agitated in light and love. Just *see* the light and love surrounding them. It's amazing how this can immediately change a person's demeanor.

I've done this myself many times, including in subways when I can feel a situation brewing. You can actually see someone all of a sudden calm down. One man I had quietly "surrounded" in light suddenly looked confused and then hurried off the train. I caution you never to stare at someone directly when you are doing this; always be discreet.

What Makes Heal From Within© Different?

I think conventional meditation as a stress management tool is flawed because, once again, we are asking the all-powerful brain to do more work. We are giving an already-stressed brain more mindful techniques to self-regulate.

Conventional meditation asks the brain to calm and empty itself by focusing on the basics like mindful breathing, expressing gratitude, and thinking happy and positive thoughts. These are fundamentals that already live inside of us. If we aren't able to feel them, it's because something is not allowing us to attain these states naturally and effortlessly.

Focusing your energy on these basic tasks further depletes your mental gas tanks. This leaves you with less "gas" for the demanding tasks that do really require your brain—like learning, working, school, organizing and creating.

With even less Qi in your tank, you are unable to handle other stressors and become stuck in a catch-22. No wonder our children are experiencing more stress than ever. Not only do they see it in us, their caretakers, but during the most expansive time of their mental development, their brains are being overtaxed with extraneous focusing.

Why does Heal From Within© work so well in overcoming mental and emotional stress? By not allowing the brain to be the sole decision maker, you can make better decisions for your overall well-being. In the training process of learning how to pause your brain, I generally avoid asking you to visualize during the Qigong, which uses mental energy. With your brain less active, you can begin to open up the gateway to your spiritual center that has been largely ignored in much of our modern society.

You've heard of IQ (intelligence quotient) and EQ (emotional quotient), but probably not QQ, what I like to call the Qi Quotient. Heal From Within© uses the language of Qi and Qigong as the tool to build your QQ.

A strong Qi Quotient will fill the spirit, calm the emotions, strengthen the physical body and subdue the brain. You no longer have to be mindful about breathing—or gaining compassion, peace and happiness either—because when you are in balance, you will feel what already lives in the spiritual center. This is when really interesting sensations will start to happen!

Let's hear how Cindy, Molly and Jonathan found HFW© to differ from other self-help techniques:

Hear how Cindy finds HFW© so much easier than the Chakra systems she had learned - 58 sec.

Molly talks about how, unlike other programs, her motivation was her continued improvement in her health and relationships - 1:19 min.

Watch Jonathan share how the spiritual aspect of this program finally connected all the dots for him - 46 sec.

I am Qi Qigong

Practice this Qigong daily, preferably at the start of your day. This mantra is paired with I am Qi and will boost the power of this Qigong when said aloud during your practice:

I am Qi
Qi flows through me
Qi surrounds me
Qi connects me
Qi empowers me
Qi is me

The stance taught in I am Qi is the basic stance for most standing Qigong exercises. This relaxed, natural position allows your Qi to flow most easily through the body.

One last reminder: When doing any of the Qigong exercises, don't worry about feeling the Qi, because the life force is always there and working for you whether you feel it or not. This is why you always feel better after doing it.

Let's practice I am Qi - 6:07 min.

Codes for Step 1 – Balancing The 4 Energy Centers

Practice I Am Qi to download these codes to the cellular level of your body.

1. I will live easier by learning to use and balance all 4 energy centers.
2. I will Release, Restore and Return to relinquish my dictator brain to let it rest during the program lessons and exercises.

Common Questions From Beginners

Why do we do Qigong daily?
Qi cannot be intellectualized; it can only be cultivated with energetic practice. Without regular practice, you cannot build your QQ. All this knowledge will just sit in the brain, continuing to stress it and feed into its dictatorship.

We are constantly being hit with external stresses and distractions, so we need something strong in order to offset them on a daily basis. Don't we sharpen our minds, nourish our bodies with good food, and show love and gratitude every day? The spirit is no different; it needs to be similarly nourished daily. Otherwise, your spirit will be weak—the same way your body reacts after you eat poorly for several days or stop exercising.

When is the best time to do my Qigong?
Anytime is fine, but the start of the day is ideal. Filling up your Qi tank in the morning will leave you in a calm but

energized state, allowing you to manage whatever the day may bring with more ease and clarity. If you do this practice consistently, you will also not feel completely depleted by the end of the day.

How do I get good at this?

The same way anybody gets good at anything: Practice, practice, practice. When you do Qigong regularly, it creates positive health benefits like better sleep, less stress and anxiety and more energy. And like any hygiene practice, when you stop, you will not feel as good or as healthy.

As the Qi builds with practice, you will feel it more quickly and powerfully. In theory, there is no right or wrong stance or technique in HFW© Qigong. As long as you feel the benefit of the Qi, then it is right for you. The suggestions given are based on my studies with various masters, and, over time, I have modified them to what worked best for me. I suggest you always try to start with my recommendation and, over time, adjust as you choose. Always do what feels right for you.

How much practice is ideal for Qigong?

Start with 10 minutes a day and gradually work up to 20 minutes. Just like when I first started exercising: I started with 15-20 minutes a couple of times a week. As my strength and endurance increased, I wanted to do more and gradually worked up to 30-40 minutes several times a week.

How do I manage when I'm too busy?

If you find that the 10 minutes of Qigong is not enough to maintain your zen, you may want to either increase the duration or frequency. You can also supplement with some Qi Breaths throughout the day. When you are super-busy or going through a particularly stressful period, the more Qi you need to stay strong and help you manage everything as calmly, productively and healthily as possible. Just like when you go on a long road trip, you need to stop and fill up your gas tank more often. When you run on empty, you will waste more time wrestling with and addressing your ailments.

Always remember, no matter how long you do the Qigong for, the most important thing is to get your brain out of the way and allow Qi to move freely. A quick 5-10 minutes of unobstructed Qi can provide tremendous benefits.

What does Qi feel like?
Most people feel relaxed and calm when Qi courses through their bodies. Some other sensations you may feel are: tingly, floating, warm or cool. You may even see colors or images. The sensations you feel are unique to how energy travels through your body and is based on many factors, including your mindset and state of your well-being. Like my acupuncture clients: in one session, they may feel exhilarated and the next fatigued because the Qi provides what is needed to balance them at that moment.

And some deeper questions:

What does connecting to the spiritual center feel like?
I am often asked. *This is what I felt or saw; is that normal?* Anything goes because each person is unique, and their interaction with Qi will also be unique. What is universal is this: the spiritual center is always a place where you will

feel loved, safe, peaceful, whole and connected. To date, my clients still can't quite describe the magnitude of this feeling in words.

It is my belief that the spirit's language of Qi is one that can only be experienced. I have a student who says that when she does her Qigong, sometimes she sees a green field and other times just a beautiful sky, but what she sees always evokes happiness and peace. What's important is that she doesn't consciously visualize these scenes; the images simply appear. The most important aspect of HFW© Qigong is that it is "mindless." Do not expend any mental energy while practicing!

When you are doing Qigong, allow the mind, body and emotions to be free to think and feel as they want. If your mind races or your heart feels anxious, don't try to rein them in. You want no resistance when doing your Qigong. Instead, as the Qi builds and flows freely, these sensations will gradually flow through you and fade.

How do you know if you are living a spiritually connected life?
Some will say they pray and go to church, synagogue or mosque regularly, they abide by the rituals and restrictions laid out by their religion, and they are charitable. But does any of this mean you are living spiritually? Not necessarily.

When you are living spiritually, you feel more at peace, content and happy despite what is going on in the world around you. If you are not feeling this way, it just means that you haven't allowed spirit in to guide you. I'm here to help you bridge that gap.

When you are feeling anxious, depressed, stressed, fearful or insecure, there's nothing wrong or bad about you. These feelings just mean that you are out of balance. I'm not saying that life will always be easy, but if you allow your spirit to guide you, you will be able to tip the scales and feel at peace more often than not.

Chapter 2 - Emotional Freedom

Reminders:

- *Before engaging with the Heal From Within© teachings and exercises, always check your brain.*
- *During Chapter 2, begin your practice with I Am Qi along with the Personal Space Opening (the beginning routine for every Qigong) and Qi Breath.*
- *Consistent daily practice is necessary to build your QQ to balance your 4 energy centers and disempower the dictator brain.*

We have discussed why you are not going to think or reason your way to overcoming stress, anxiety and depression, no matter how smart, educated or accomplished you are. You have tried these mental gymnastics for years, and they haven't worked. You can already see that this is an entirely new approach.

Thankfully, you have many protective mechanisms at your disposal to keep you safe. Your body offers warnings (pain, rapid heartbeat) to alert you to danger. You have an inner voice that guides you to act in your best interest to keep you safe and healthy. Many people believe that this inner voice lives inside the brain. But how can this be true if the brain that drives you mad is in the same place your protective and comforting inner voice resides? This would be a flawed design or a contradiction in logic, causing you a lot of confusion in life.

This is why I suggest our inner voice does not live inside our brains and why we need to "check our brain" so we can hear our intuitive and instinctive signals with less interference. With our brain in idle mode, we can begin our journey to emotional freedom by cleaning out the energetic cobwebs of our past that have caused us great pain, shame and suffering.

My Own Freedom

Qigong is the only practice that allowed me to shut down my logical, overthinking mind—a feat that seemed impossible. With my mind at bay, I was able to let Qi's intelligence release the grip of the negative energetic buildup in my body. My soul's voice was revealed once again and returned me back to my previous aware and strong state after my *14-year* health crisis.

Before we begin, I would like to share a bit more of my own story. I do this to highlight how this practice can not only liberate you but give you full control over how you choose to experience your life. The teacher before you on the video clips is a result of this program. I hope that I can inspire you to feel that you can easily learn these tools to overcome any difficulty you may have (or have had) in your own life.

I mentioned that I was the first member of my family to go to a four-year university. But all was not rosy just because I'd left home. As a sophomore, I was given a date rape drug, and although I don't have full clear memories of everything that happened that night, I do know I was sexually violated.

I share this incident not because this is an inspirational memoir about how my internal strength and perseverance allowed me to triumph. I am certainly not going to give you hollow rhetoric and tell you that you, too, can overcome similar traumas by just being strong. Yes, I was strong enough to overcome this assault as well ... I had to be to overcome my early years. But teaching *how you can acquire* more internal strength is what's important.

Growing up, I never allowed myself to get sidetracked by external noise, material attractions and triviality. I instinctively knew the necessity of letting go of the emotional residue of all the unfortunate events in my life. I didn't leave these emotions bottled up inside of me to cloud my judgment, keep me stuck in the past and prevent me from moving forward and seizing life the way I wanted to.

But what I know now is that my soul was leading me all along. The soul is wise beyond comprehension and helps us navigate and learn through life's challenges.

During the development of this program, I retold many of my life stories to my husband and friends. They usually remarked that they had forgotten a lot of these major events in my life. Why? Because I don't live with or carry their emotional weight, and they see only what I've become as opposed to my burdensome past. To be honest, sometimes I myself forget the details of the worst events of my early years—because the trauma no longer lives in me.

People often ask me if I'm really as calm inside as I appear to be. It is not a persona; I usually feel naturally calm. That's not to say I live in this state 24/7. I am human and susceptible to the emotional roller coaster of life. That was certainly the case when I lost my sleep for 14 years.

My belief is that the best teacher is one who lives by the principles they teach and has experienced these issues first-hand. That's why all the sponsors in AA programs are recovering alcoholics. The most effective coaches are the ones who have had success in overcoming a particular problem or ailment. Why? Because having gone through it themselves, they know the formula for success.

I've been called wise my entire life, but I am now sure that this wisdom lives in all of us. I was fortunate enough to be born with the innate ability not to allow the emotions of my traumas to build up inside. Had I not possessed this ability, the pressure cooker of pain and sadness in my early years would have drowned out the voice of my wise soul.

Clearing Negative Emotions

In this chapter, we will focus on clearing the energetic charge from your negative emotions. Anger, guilt, shame, sorrow, grief, fear and worry are just some of the feelings that create negative tensions that you can't shake. Such toxic emotions can result from any encounter or event that is currently affecting you, memories of the past, or things that haven't even happened yet, but you may dread facing.

Whatever your situation may be, these teachings and the Qigong practice will help you loosen the grips these emotions have on your mind and body and allow you to move forward in a more clear state. Qigong is quite simply the best practice to clear any heightened emotional energy from your body.

Instinct vs. Intuition

Some equate intuition with instinct. Instinct is an innate impulse to act to safeguard our survival. It is a primitive animal drive that kicks in to protect ourselves or act upon danger.

Intuition is an innate sense of knowing and wisdom that is not developed through the consciousness. Intuition is the ability to receive information from outside the brain; it comes from your soul's higher sense of perception. Instinct cannot be learned, whereas intuition is something that can be cultivated over time with the language of Qi. Don't worry if this seems far-reaching to you. You are learning a new language, but this energetic language already exists inside of you. We are just defining and giving a name to it. As you allow Qi to clear the blockages in your body, you will begin to access the intuition from your spiritual center.

Emotional Baggage

The first thing to recognize is that it's not the events in your life that bog you down. It's the energetic charge from your reactions to those events that you carry around. These negative energies are heavy and take up a lot of space inside your body, creating toxins that cause you distress. You can suppress these reactions and even hide them from the outside world, but you cannot fool the body.

Too often, once a painful or traumatic event is over, your emotional reactions to it remain inside you for much too long. There is no purpose served or any good that comes from holding onto these negative feelings for a prolonged period of time.

I had a patient in her early 30s who had cervical cancer. By the time she came to me, she had lost 30 pounds, couldn't eat and was debilitated from the cancer treatments, which she, unfortunately, wasn't responding well to. Every time I worked on her, I felt tremendous blockages in her lower abdomen. Even gently touching that area would evoke a great deal of discomfort. I asked her about it several times, and she said that she was concerned about how the cancer treatments would affect her fertility—she wanted to have kids in the future. I felt that there was more to this, but obviously, she wasn't ready to share it.

During our sessions, she would comment how the energy shifts felt like a war was going on inside her body, often leaving her very drained. Unfortunately, she continued to not respond well to her Western drugs. She decided to take some time off before possibly embarking on new drug therapies. The last time I saw her, she divulged to me that she had been gang-raped at age 18. I realized at that moment that I could never help others release what I cannot access. And even if she had told me earlier that she had been gang-raped, how could I release the toxic memory in her body without her awareness and assistance in this energetic process?

LESSON: People around you can't help you release the turmoil you keep inside. It is easier for you to learn how to release your own pain than it is for someone else to do it for you, which is impossible. Clearing the heavy, dark leftover energy will break the connection between the physical, mental and emotional memories and allow the deep healing process to begin.

Let's hear how Molly understands her body's signals to help her know when she is out of balance – 2:23 min.

Effect of Emotions on Your Productivity

There is nothing positive about negative feelings. Some people become accustomed to their negative emotions; they've been living with them for so long that it's almost become part of their DNA. I have people who come to me for stress relief and then admit that they believe their worries or fears actually protect them from bad things happening.

I've heard others say that sometimes anxiety or stress motivates them to be more productive. I think that's because they don't realize how much more productive they would be without it, not to mention much happier and healthier. Think about it: if you were hiring someone, who would you want to work for you? Someone who can produce efficiently from a clear, neutral state or someone who constantly allows life to get in the way of their work?

We are inefficient when we have emotional clutter. If we first have to work through layers of self-doubt, anger, depression, anxiety, fear and insecurities, every task takes longer. These negative emotions compromise our judgment and prevent us from putting our best work out there.

Think about living in a cluttered home or office. In order to accomplish a chore, you first have to wade through and move all of this mess which becomes very inefficient and tiring. The same thing happens when you live with baggage in your heart and mind. Every time you need to resolve an issue—or even in some cases when you are simply trying to enjoy yourself—you first have to push your way through doubts and self-deprecating thoughts.

Marie Kondo is a renowned organizational consultant. After many years of helping people organize their clutter, it dawned on her that we don't want or need to organize the things we no longer need in our life. We can simply free ourselves of it.

Her book *The Life-Changing Magic of Tidying Up* teaches you how to declutter your home. Clearing your living space means there's less junk to maneuver around, which allows you to live in a home filled with only positive energy. I adopted her program in my own house, and the result was very liberating. And just like HFW©, this is not a one-time cleaning but a continual process.

As so beautifully and clearly stated by Marie, "Start by discarding all at once, intensely and completely. Keep only those things that speak to your heart. The question of what to own is actually the question of how you want to live your life."

After clearing your emotional baggage, you will start to feel more space in your mind, heart and body, similar to the spacious feeling of a decluttered home. With this renewed clarity of mind, your improved productivity translates to gaining back some much-needed free time.

There is so much talk these days about not having enough time. If only I could add more hours to the day to accomplish all that I need to do. I want to not only give you more time but help you enjoy whatever free time you do have.

Most people think improved productivity comes from clearing the mind, but calming the heart is what is needed first.

Let's hear how Suzy feels after taking out the energetic trash from her daily life - 2:15 min.

With a still heart comes a clearer mind, allowing us to become more efficient at handling tasks with ease and proficiency. Without emotional burdens weighing you down, you can move through life more efficiently and effectively. You will have less mental clutter to go through, which will free up your time each day to do the things that make you happy and are truly meaningful in your life.

The State of the Heart

This step is not about managing negative emotions (fear, stress, anger, grief). Manage or organize only those things in your life that you want to keep (spouse, kids, money, house, job, friends). If you are managing the negative, this means that you are keeping this energy inside of you.

If you are not resolving your problems, they remain problems.

Nor is this step about feeling positive all the time. We're humans. On many occasions we will feel hurt, angry or even depressed. Emotions are a natural part of living; they help us express what our body is experiencing (both negative and positive). Once they have served their purpose, it's important not to allow these emotions to stay bottled up inside, where they can paralyze us. We want to transform them so we can get back to a clear state. This will help us gain the proper perspective, one that allows us to move forward.

The state of the heart determines how you approach each situation. If your fear or anxiety about a certain situation (such as a job interview, getting lost) overwhelms you, then your ability to deal with that situation is diminished, making it even more difficult and challenging. Picture a general on the front lines who is anxious and fearful—he would probably not win us the war. You want a clear-headed commander at the helm. It's always best to discharge any heightened emotions, so you can then assess and address any situation with a cool head.

Return to Your Soul Qigong

Return to Your Soul will help you clear the negative emotional charge around any situation, whether it be current, past or even future events. Once the energetic charge is cleared, you then allow the Qi to help you become aligned in perfect harmony with the given situation. In this calm and balanced state, your soul's wisdom can give you the necessary perspective to make peace with whatever is confronting you.

Return to Your Soul has a wide range of applications:

- Clear negative emotions immediately from the body (anger, fear, sadness, anxiety, worry).
- Resolve conflicts (present and even long-standing ones), for example, in a work situation, or a marriage, improve character flaws in yourself.

- Receive guidance on any situation that you feel confused, stressed, anxious, or conflicted about, such as how to find love, how to improve a relationship.

Do Return to Your Soul on an as-needed basis, as many times as necessary, to prevent your negative emotions from accumulating. If, at the end of the day, you still have some residual emotional tension, do this Qigong before bedtime, so your body can fully rest and regenerate.

There are two parts to this Qigong.

Part 1 - Stilling the Heart

This is where you will clear the energetic charge of an issue you are having difficulty with. There are many tapping techniques that clear emotional energy from the body (like Neuro-Emotional Technique-NET and Emotional Freedom Technique-EFT), but this is the most powerful one I have discovered. I learned this Song Kong Tong technique from Master Peng, and it works quickly and effectively.

1. Begin by acknowledging the issue you are having difficulty with. The issue might be an event that happened today, in the past or lies in the future—anything that is causing you concern, confusion, disturbance, anxiety, fear or any other negative feeling. There is no need to dwell or focus on the issue—just quickly recall it.
2. You will then tap the top of the head while chanting 6 times:

Song Kong Tong
Bing Chuan Yu

3. Repeat the chant 6 times as you tap the entry point for each of the dantians: First the Upper Dantian (between the eyebrows), then the Middle Dantian (between the breasts on the sternum) and then the Lower Dantian (right below the navel). Do not worry about enunciating the chant perfectly.

Song Kong Tong means to relax, open and embody the divine energy.

Bing Chuan Yu means to dissipate the energetic charge around an issue and reorganize it in a perfect compassionate pattern.

The only intent in this part of the Qigong is to let the energy come in to relax, open your channels, release the charge and get you into a perfectly balanced and aligned state at the present moment.

Part 2 - Window to the Soul

Part 2 is a supplement that I added to Master Peng's original chant. After you have gotten rid of the emotional charge around the situation, you will sit quietly for a short period to let the intelligence of the Qi do its work while you enjoy your calm state. The intent is to gain the necessary perspective from your wise voice so that you can best manage the situation.

The difficulty the brain has in recognizing the elusive soul is what prevents most people from benefiting from this part of the Qigong. Without this awareness, they will go back to the habit of *resorting to the brain for answers*. For now, until the soul becomes clearer to you, be patient, stay open to these new communications and sensations and see where they lead you. Know that you are getting back in touch with the truth already inside of you, wherever it may live.

It is important not to activate the mind by ruminating about the situation. You only want to observe it like a third party. Feel yourself floating above your body and the issue. Observe your 5 natural senses: Watch, listen, feel, hear and smell without the brain trying to dominate with its own judgment or interpretation. If the mind wanders, don't control it or try to rein it in. Over time, as your spiritual Qi develops and your trust along with it, its power will quell the chatter of the mind.

Allow any communication, sensation or perceptions to be revealed to you. These cannot be forced, but when received will give you an immediate sense of truth, realization or knowing without further need for interpretation.

I had a client who told me she saw a horse during one of her Qigong exercises. She didn't understand it and said this image was weird, because she doesn't ride or even like horses. I asked her what the horse was doing. She said running. I asked her what a running horse meant to her. She looked at me and said, "Ohhh... freedom." She knew immediately what it meant for her. Her soul had shown her in its own language. Two years later, she got a divorce.

Remember, when doing Return to Your Soul, you are asking the soul to help you understand how you can come to terms with a situation. I have had clients tell me that they ask, "How can I get my husband/daughter/friend to see or change..." These types of questions will likely not elicit any feedback because we can't control anyone except ourselves.

Even when there is no discernible communication from the soul, there are positive effects as a result of your calm state. You can see the situation with a clearer perspective, and your energy shift may change the dynamics—the issue might suddenly seem to resolve itself. But never have expectations of anything happening after Return to Your Soul. Just Allow.

AN IMPORTANT NOTE: Your truth and all communications from within are always good and pure. If you ever feel the urge to do something bad or harmful to yourself or others, it is not your soul speaking, and you must seek medical attention immediately. People tend to laugh when I say this, but I do feel like I need to put this disclaimer out there. To date, no client of mine has ever received any kind of negative communication, but you never know.

You may do this exercise standing, sitting or lying down.

Let's discharge, reorganize and connect to our inner voice with Return to Your Soul - 4:48 min.

Soul Training Exercise

Window to the Soul is definitely the most challenging aspect of the Qigong for some. Spending time nurturing your spirit is not the difficult part—that's just sitting and observing your 5 natural senses, getting in touch with yourself and how and what you feel. The difficulty lies in learning to trust the soul and its communications and be led by them.

After you have done Return to Your Soul, you may still have difficulty sensing the soul communicating through your body or are unable to interpret its signals. Let's follow up with a simple soul-training exercise. After this Qigong, frame your conflict into a question with only 2 defined answers: yes or no, black or red, this or that, should I or shouldn't I. Now sense how your body reacts to both answers. Then act on the answer that gives your body an immediate calm and knowing sensation. Let your body show you the truth that makes you feel aligned and balanced in the moment. This can give you some comfort in moving forward one way or the other without remaining stuck in angst and struggle.

Please understand that any communication you receive from your soul is not a guarantee of the outcome you want. Sometimes what you are led to do is just a necessary step on the path to your bigger goal(s). The more you continue this work, and the more you learn about yourself, the clearer it will become what it is you truly want and need and how to attain it.

Even though this soul training exercise helps you to listen to your body answer binary questions (yes or no, this or that), we know that many situations in life cannot be solved that simply. Some situations offer many choices; others are not black or white but gray and complicated. But this can guide you step by step.

This soul training exercise is best done after Return to Your Soul when your heart is still, and you are in alignment and harmony with the universe. Without being in that state, your dominating brain may interfere with the body's sensations.

Each of us comes into Heal From Within© at a different place in our life, at varying levels of mental, emotional, physical and spiritual development. Remember, there is no timeline to learning about yourself. You do not need to feel that connecting to your spiritual center requires master-level training or that you must dedicate lots of time and radical change to your lifestyle to live in peace.

I do 15-30 minutes of Qigong a day, and most of my clients succeed while doing less than that. However, you do need to exercise your spirit a little bit every day and let it have a say in your life. Every Qi sensation you feel gets you one step closer to your soul.

Let's hear Ann discuss how this work is unique and different for each person - 45 sec.

Codes for Step 2 – Emotional Freedom

Use Return to Your Soul to download these codes to the cellular level of your body.

1. I will not become attached to my extreme emotions. Instead, I will clear them from my life and body.
2. I am ready to Release my stuck energy and Restore to free flow and balance in order to Return to my soul for guidance.

Chapter 3 - Self Empowerment

Reminders:

- *Before engaging with the Heal From Within© teachings and exercises, always check your brain.*
- *During Chapter 3, release as much emotional baggage as possible with Return to Your Soul.*
- *Continue doing I Am Qi in the morning along with the Personal Space Opening (the beginning routine for every Qigong).*

You are more powerful than you know; you are beautiful just as you are.

- Melissa Etheridge

Whether you think you can or can't, you're right.

- Henry Ford

It is never too late to be who you might have been.

- George Eliot

It is during our darkest moments that we must focus to see the light.

- Aristotle Onassis

These are all inspiring quotes—some of my favorites—but how do you "just do it" if you don't truly believe in your own strength? I want to do more than inspire you with pithy motivational sayings. I want you to use tangible energetic tools so you can *feel* the greatness inside you instead of having to constantly pump yourself up!

Now that you have begun to clear the built-up negative emotions in your body, you can start to empower and live from your strong inner self by building up the Qi in your Spiritual Center.

We all come into this world with certain predispositions or inherited energy passed on from previous generations. Some people are more emotional, others completely logical. Some are prone to anxiety, depression and fearfulness, while others are naturally bold and confident. Regardless of your energetic inheritance, this energy is not fixed. It is something that can be balanced and improved upon.

You can have complete control over yourself, regardless of your predispositions. Undesirable traits are malleable, and with the help of Qi and your spiritual center, you can make some remarkable changes. You just need to keep the energy flowing freely, so your spiritual center guides you as much as your mental one.

Your negative energies create blockages that make it hard for you to change your life, so you develop coping mechanisms to compensate. Let's say you injured your right knee, and you start to lean more on the left leg to compensate. This could cause you to develop bad posture as a result, plus compensatory pain in the other previously unaffected parts of your body.

As I have mentioned, modern scientists and doctors believe that mental and emotional reactions to certain experiences create neural pathways in our brains. The strongest reactions will create the most dominant neural pathways, which then affect behavior and habits. Let's say a boy cruelly dumps a girl publicly and with no warning. This negative experience leaves her feeling humiliated and unwanted. Unfortunately, the girl may continue to relive these uncomfortable feelings because our negative-biased brains not only register negative events more readily but also tend to dwell on them.

This one event could set the girl's dominant neural pathway to one of living with a lack of confidence and a negative self-image. She may then bring this insecurity into all of her future relationships. With each subsequent failure, she creates a self-fulfilling prophecy. In the world of Qi, I see her experience and reactions as causing negative energy, and without effective ways to transform it, remaining stuck in her body.

Conventional Western thought suggests that you can change neural pathways and create healthier new habits with regular repetition of positive thinking, feelings and actions. This is challenging because, as humans, we are constantly swimming against the tide of negativity. How many positive conscious thoughts would we need to change even one behavior within our predisposed negative-biased brains? This is a constant battle, one in which the negative autopilot will naturally win over our arduous conscious efforts to "think positively."

This is why my approach to balance the brain requires you to bypass it entirely; you do not want to fight through its resistance. Instead, address the stuck Qi directly. If your garden has lots of rocks covering up the soil, the first thing you do is clear the rocks and then fertilize with good nutrients.

Often the root causes for certain behaviors have been suppressed for a long time. We only try to address them once these behaviors begin to cause us undue stress or illness. We may not even be aware of the root problem; these issues have caused us so much pain that we have subconsciously suppressed them to avoid facing them. But nothing good comes from suppressing or ignoring problems. The past always catches up with us eventually, in health and in life.

Even with the stuck Qi removed, we still must ultimately understand the core issue in order to address, overcome and prevent it from happening again. Only by completely resolving the underlying issues can we move forward in health and strength.

Heal From Within©'s 3R process of returning you to a free-flowing and aligned state paves the way for you to gain clarity on how to balance any faulty or compensatory behaviors with the help of your united 4 energy centers.

To work the three 3R process successfully, you need to first recognize that you can change the behavioral patterns that prevent your Qi from flowing freely.

The only thing we truly have control over is ourselves, so that is where we always start and return to.

Reboot Your System

Now you are going to see the nerdy techie computer programmer side of me! I often think in a logical and systematic manner, which is how I designed the HFW© program.

Ann says that the program's systematic approach is one of its greatest strengths - 1:21 min.

To understand the elusive concept of how HFW© Qigong works, let's start with a quick computer lesson.

Hardware refers to the physical components of a computer: the monitor, CPU, keyboard, mouse, etc. Software has no physical presence; its programs are developed to tell a computer system what to do: operating system, apps, etc. Operating systems (Windows, macOS, Android) are the most important piece of software in a computer; they run in the background managing the hardware, memory and other system processes. Computer apps (Word, iTunes, Maps, Instagram) are software that helps you use your computer.

Hardware is, for the most part, fixed, and although you can make minor upgrades, each component has a limited life span, like all machines. Operating systems and apps, however, are just codes; they are not fixed and can be modified at any time as long as you know the language.

I studied computer science in college and built software programs for 12 years in my previous computer consulting career. I modified countless codes to fix bugs and improve performance. As a healer, I use this computer analogy to explain how to reset your neural pathways—that is, how to fix your bugs and upgrade your life.

In humans, the hardware is the physical body we inherited and were born with: skin, hair, organs, bones, etc.

Although we can tweak or even replace some parts, for the most part, we have to live within our physical boundaries. And one day, our body will expire, just like a computer.

Our operating system (OS) contains our personality traits and core beliefs. They're inherited at birth and dictate how we manage our bodies and live our life. Our OS runs in the background and helps us navigate our health and well-being. Our personality and beliefs operate on a subconscious level and are further shaped by our experiences and cultural influences, such as religion and society at large.

Our apps contain the behaviors that help us interact with the outside world, which are developed based on our beliefs and personality (OS). Our OS and apps are energetic codes and mostly not questioned by us until they start causing problems in our lives—like depression, anxiety or my mom's mental breakdown.

In summary:

	Fixed Hardware	(Upgradable) Software Codes	
		Operating System (OS)	Apps
Computer	monitor, CPU, keyboard, mouse	Windows, macOS, Android	Word, iTunes, Maps, Instagram
Human	skin, hair, organs, bones	Personality traits, principles, beliefs, values	Behavior: argumentative, cooperative, ambitious, lazy

Operating systems and apps are constantly being upgraded on a computer. We are all familiar with the message you get on your computer or phone: "Updates ready to install." These code changes correct bugs, improve performance or add enhanced features to help the entire computer system run more efficiently with fewer errors. In this chapter, you will learn how you can "update" some of your less-desirable beliefs and behaviors.

Our positive personality traits (self-reliant, humorous, creative, logical) are essential to our survival. In comparison, the negative ones (depressive, anxious, mistrusting) are detrimental to our well-being. The positive aspects of our OS are the lifeline to our well-being and must be continually nourished, while the less desirable ones do not serve us and can be upgraded. Some schools of thought contend that certain core morals and beliefs—the convictions that seemingly would be learned, such as "trust no one" or "you can control your own fate"—might also be passed down through our ancestors.

I believe certain aspects of our OS are inherited as karmic codes. Karma is known as "what goes around comes around," but the most important part of karma is that it means "action." It is important to realize that it is your actions (or maybe those of your ancestors) that created an effect and not some outside force. Therefore, it is entirely within your power to create new karmic behaviors and actions.

What's important to understand is that your behavior apps (meek, respectful, aggressive, impudent) express your OS of beliefs. Before you can change these apps, you must change the OS that influences these actions. For example, if you believe people are inherently dishonest, you must first change this perception to correct your combative and worried behavior that stems from this belief.

Otherwise, focusing your efforts on some of the typical self-help tips, such as being present, breathing, and grateful, will not be very productive. You may feel a bit daunted at the idea of transforming your inherited energy, but I assure you that HFW© is a seamless, easy and uplifting process. With the help of Qigong, you can transform your Qi to upgrade certain traits and beliefs to create new behaviors.

One of my students carried a great deal of anger inside. She said, "It runs in my family. My mom and grandmother were like this too, and I just can't control my anger with my twins many times." Some would say that she observed this behavior all her life and adopted it. Others would say she inherited this predisposition towards angry outbursts. I say since it's not hard-wired and it does not serve her well-being, she can change it. She was able to make great improvements with this program.

Qigong is the tool that will help upgrade your beliefs and traits (OS) to bring about a new set of behaviors (apps), empowering you to live your personal best.

Here's what Jonathan has to say about the seamless and easy process of HFW© - 36 sec.

When my daughter was in preschool, Dr. Robert Brooks had just written a book called *Raising Resilient Children.* I loved the title, so I went to see him speak. He said one thing that changed the way I parented; that we run certain negative scripts (which I call apps) throughout our life and never change them, *even when they don't produce the outcome we want.*

He cites, as an example, how we constantly tell our kids to clean up their rooms. They don't listen, but we keep saying it over and over again from the time they are 5 years old till they leave for college. Dr. Brooks says if that script hasn't worked in 13 years, it never will—so either change the script or don't go into your kid's room anymore. From that day forward, I never got stuck on one method if it didn't work. I firmly believed in what Dr. Brooks said.

This philosophy applies to the rest of my life as well, including my private healing practice. I hear from many people who say they've been practicing a certain modality, taking a supplement or seeing an acupuncturist regularly for a year. When I ask them if it's working, they say, "I think so, but maybe it will just take a little more time for real results." If something hasn't begun to make improvements in 6 months or a year, I don't believe it ever will. When you perform the correct treatment or prescribe the right herbal formula, your body will feel a noticeable improvement within a reasonable timeframe. If you don't feel a positive change after a few of my sessions, I reevaluate and either do something new or refer out.

I apply this philosophy to my personal life as well. Is what I'm doing working for me? Am I feeling good about myself? Are my relationships going well? When I find myself in a negative pattern, I take a moment to reflect inwardly and evaluate what's keeping me there. Then I change it! If something is not working for me, I know I can find a new script that will.

Over the years, I have seen many people who come in and say, "Heal me. I hear you are a magician. I hear acupuncture helps people with anxiety or depression." I'm sorry to say that I have no magical powers, although some people are convinced I do. I have come to realize that what many of these people are really saying is, "I want to stay the same, living the same stressed-out life, but I want you to do something to fix me." That is an ineffective band-aid approach.

We look for external fixes without committing to internal change.

Many people who are unhappy or stressed will blame their problems on external factors, like their job or living situation. They may feel the need to switch jobs, retire, or move to a new home and city. However, when unhappiness and stress come from within, a move will only bring momentary relief. Believing that your happiness is dependent on external factors will keep you trying to control the world around you—which is futile.

What happens if you get a new boss and your dream job turns out not to be so dreamy? What happens if your new house turns into a money pit? You are right back to feeling stressed and unhappy. If you can't change your external situation, are you doomed to stay stressed and unhappy forever?

The surest way to overcome any problem is to change the only thing you have absolute control over, and that is you.

Your Qi is the magic.

Always remember that peace and happiness are natural states that come as a result of your actions. It is fruitless to try to convince yourself to just "be happy." If you are not living as happily and peacefully as you would like, the question is simply, Why? Followed by, What is causing it? Let's correct the internal, so you aren't dependent on the uncontrollable external world to make you whole.

Self-Awareness Exercise

Self-awareness—the ability to see yourself clearly and understand how your thoughts, feelings, values, strengths and weaknesses impact the world around you—is a critical aspect of your internal work. The more self-aware you are, the more likely you are to feel happier, be satisfied in your career and relationships and feel more in control over every aspect of your life. Conversely, a lack of self-awareness can lead to more anxiety, stress and depression.

A buildup of negative energy impedes your ability to look inward and enjoy this awareness. Without a clear inner perspective, you may be left wondering why your relationships are filled with strife.

Internal introspection is difficult for many people because the idea of facing your flaws head-on can be scary. Examining yourself in this manner is challenging when your negative brain is at the helm. However, if you let your soul lead the process, you do not feel berated or chastised. Instead, the soul lovingly guides you to let go of patterns or behaviors that have gotten in the way of returning to your personal truth, beauty, strength and happiness.

Many years ago, before HFW©, I came up with this self-awareness exercise for my daughter during some challenging times in both of our lives.

Part 1: Let's create 6 groups of relationships with people that you interact with the most often in your daily life: for example, partner, parent, children, friend, employee, employer, student, teacher.

For each group, list 3-5 characteristics or qualities that you admire, value or expect from these people (for example, what ideal qualities would you want from your partner (a spouse or significant other), parent, child, sibling, friend, boss? These are qualities you would like to see in them—not ones they necessarily possess. If you don't currently have a partner, but would like one, include them as one of your groups.

There are certainly some characteristics that will be the same across the groups, but there are probably some qualities you may value in a co-worker that you may not need in a partner.

Remember, we do this exercise not to judge ourselves or anyone else; this is a "check" so we can recalibrate if we need to.

Relationship 1: __________

Desirable traits: __________ __________ __________

__________ __________ __________

Relationship 2: __________

Desirable traits: __________ __________ __________

__________ __________ __________

Relationship 3: __________

Desirable traits: __________ __________ __________

__________ __________ __________

Relationship 4: __________

Desirable traits: __________ __________ __________

__________ __________ __________

Relationship 5: __________

Desirable traits: __________ __________ __________

__________ __________ __________

Relationship 6: _________

Desirable traits: _________ _________ _________

_________ _________ _________

Let's take a look at your results.

Here are some of the more common characteristics I have received from clients.

1. Significant other: Grounded, Sexy, Humorous, Good Role Model, Dependable, Forgiving, Trustworthy, Committed Partnership
2. Parent: Supportive, Integrity, Loving, Intelligent, Consistent, Patient, Trustworthy, Adoration
3. Child: Self-Confident, Honest, Curious, Independent, Optimism, Loving, Funny, Desire to Learn
4. Friend: Supportive, Good Listener, Curious, Dependable, Honest, Lack of Judgment, Availability, Creativity
5. Employer: Direct, Motivating, Smart, Vision, Stable, Supportive, Compromising, Gritty
6. Employee: Honest, Intuitive, Hardworking, Energetic, Respectful, Dependable, Self-Motivating, Able to Set and Achieve Goals

Look at your list and ask yourself: do you live up to your own standards, the ones you have defined as important in your relationships? Do you embody these same characteristics as a partner, child, parent, worker, boss, etc.?

If you note some personal characteristics you have identified as being incongruent with your standards, you have now become more consciously aware. Congratulations, this is the first step towards returning to the characteristics you admire and respect. They already live inside you.

When I did this exercise with my daughter, she learned more about her personality, strengths and weaknesses. However, because it was done purely as a mental exercise, it just made her feel bad about herself because she didn't know how to make any changes. In retrospect, without a connection to her soul to lovingly guide her through the changes she would need to make, the exercise felt punitive, highlighting all her deficiencies.

Part 2: Do a Return to Your Soul to dissipate the negative feeling around these undesired characteristics or behaviors, and allow the Qi to reorganize your energy into a perfect compassionate pattern.

1. Let your soul reveal what is holding you back from displaying the characteristic(s) that you admire in others but are not able to fully express in your own relationships.
2. Let your inner truth show you how to transform certain characteristics and/or let go of behavior(s) that do not serve you.

3. If your spiritual center hasn't been awakened yet, you may also explore these questions with a trusted family member, friend or therapist who can be honest with you and give you insights. But continue to open up to your soul. When the answer is revealed, it will feel like you dialed the right combination and the lock is open.

If you can identify characteristics that you admire and respect in others but have lost in yourself, it's time to work on these areas of your personality. Otherwise, a dark space will remain inside of you and prevent you from fully loving and trusting yourself.

If you go through this list and believe you meet all your own standards, ask yourself in which areas of your life/relationships are you having difficulty? That may be a clue that you need to transform something in that category.

After completing this exercise, one of my clients realized that he wanted to be more self-confident and more of a visionary—traits he admired in his bosses and co-workers. He realized that his lack of success in this area stemmed from his adversity to taking risks, which were caused by his fears. With the intelligence of Qi to help transform his fears, he made great strides. He allowed his soul to gently, lovingly and wisely guide him to unleash the confident visionary that already lived inside him.

We must address the root issues because living with the feeling of being an imposter or unworthy is so debilitating. Some people can bury these feelings and pretend they don't exist, but that takes a lot of energy, even if we are not conscious of it. Don't let the mind make you feel embarrassed or frightened to improve and upgrade these behaviors. Instead, let your soul show you how great you are meant to be.

What would you think of someone who overcame a personal obstacle or transformed a character flaw? You would congratulate and admire them. Why not do that for yourself?

So, let's start to clear all the skeletons in the closet. With each hurdle you overcome, the lighter and freer you will feel.

Heed the Messenger

I had a client tell me that her son felt she wasn't trustworthy. She sadly acknowledged that is true sometimes—and that was a big step. My client endured a very troubled childhood and realized that the coping skills she had been forced to employ as a child no longer needed to be in her life. She realized in this case that her son was the messenger bringing to her attention a matter that had affected her relationships for decades.

I mostly rely on my spirit to guide me, but after having my own family, I also allow my husband and kids, whom I trust and adore, to help me evolve. I'm always looking to improve, and most importantly, I have the willingness and belief that I can change. I then open my spirit to guide me so I can see my missteps as opportunities for personal growth instead of focusing on my shortcomings. Following the true teachings of this program, I honor any advice or suggestion if it feels right for me.

Experience Life as You Choose

Because we don't live in a bubble, let's look at how we deal with external situations and people in our lives that are beyond our control. Again… all you can change is you, so when confronted with a difficult situation, allow yourself only two choices on how to react.

1. Can you change the situation? If yes, then take the necessary steps to do just that!
2. If you can't, then change the way you experience it. Which means, how do you change your relationship with this particular situation so that you are not stuck and miserable?

Here's a practical example of how I employed this method in my childhood. As I said, I pretty much raised myself. I could have felt sorry for myself, been angry, gotten stuck in the whys and the ifs, spent my life feeling bad for myself and focused on all the things I didn't have.

Instead, I chose to change my relationship with my situation so I could live in the most empowered state possible. I was able to focus on what I did have, which was the freedom to do whatever I wanted when I wanted, which I took full advantage of. After I finished my household duties, I did what I felt like doing because I had no parents to answer to. I did have older sisters, who restricted me at times, but they left the house when I was 13, and my freedom really kicked in. I watched a lot of TV, listened to music, did puzzles, and stayed in my room reflecting a lot. Basically, I did whatever made me happy. (Shhh ... I also cut school a lot.)

At a very young age, I intuitively made the decision to be in control and not follow in my family's footsteps. For one thing, I decided I would never become too focused on money. My dad frequently talked about how life would be so much better if we had more money. I thought to myself, we would be richer and probably even more dysfunctional! I decided that if I had kids, I would do everything possible to make sure the many dysfunctions of my childhood did not carry over to my future family.

The car I bought at 17 gave me physical independence, but I had always experienced *internal freedom of choice.* I got to make my own decisions in life. And remember, no one can control your thoughts and emotions. That is all on you.

It is a big step to say I have the power to change what I don't like. Begin by taking responsibility for your life so you have complete control over how to respond and are no longer living reactively. You really do have choices, as opposed to being held captive to a situation and just hoping for change.

This is key to becoming the master of your life instead of feeling hopelessly bound to fate or your inherited limitations. Despite whatever is going on right now, you have control and don't need to rely on anybody else's decision or indecision for your own happiness.

If you always look for answers outside yourself, you will never have control over your own well-being.

Self-empowerment starts with the belief that you can write your own script because you have the freedom to experience life as you choose. Start by upgrading your OS of beliefs by installing the basic codes at the end of each chapter. These beliefs will create positive neural pathways, and your behavior (apps) will then change your relationships and interactions with the external world. And what happens next? The byproduct is living more happily, peacefully and healthfully with a lot less effort and thought.

However, be careful of falling back into your karmic rut. This is easy to do because you've been running your OS and apps throughout your entire life (and possibly your ancestors' as well.) They are so ingrained in us, and unfortunately, we live in a society that doesn't support or worship this type of inner development. Until it does, it can be hard to go against conventional standards.

A client asked me a great question once: How can one heal themselves from within and connect to their inner truth and needs if they are also connected to a partner and children with their own spirit and truth? This resonated with me; I have and still do live with that same issue. It can be challenging when those we are closest to don't share the same beliefs or the same spiritual path. Some of my clients have felt unsupported and even ridiculed by their loved ones during this journey. This is where finding a group of like-souled people (as suggested earlier) to share and support you during your journey will help you stay focused on your healing path. Our online group's members often express how happy they are to be supported by a group of people who all speak the same "Qi" language and share a common goal: to live their best lives so they can help others in the world to do the same.

As you change, you may notice that you will turn skeptics into supporters. This can lead to improvements in your relationships, and some of them may even join you on your path (as has happened with some of my clients). A few of my male clients credit HFW© for drastically improving relationships with their wives and/or children. One of the biggest blessings from this program for me personally was the strong relationship it helped my husband forge with our three girls.

Until then, do not allow anyone to sidetrack you from your goals. Live the way you want to, and let people gravitate towards you if and when they choose to. Everyone is on their own journey, and you can't control the direction they take. HFW© Qigong will keep your spirit strong and centered and help you avoid being sucked into other people's negativity. Simply focus on your practice, and you will thrive with confidence.

Permanently Installing the Codes

Once you have learned the codes at the end of every chapter, live and act on them consciously. I had a client who, after every lesson, made it a point to change her mindset and adopt these codes into her daily routine. By just reminding herself of the codes and following them consciously, she was always amazed at how much better she would feel.

However, don't stop there. Let's permanently install all the codes in this program into your OS by downloading them to a cellular, subconscious level. The only way I have found to do that successfully is to let the codes bypass the mental center. Do the HFW© Qigong daily to let Qi install them into the cellular memory of your physical center so the codes become rote.

My hope is that once your OS is upgraded and a subconscious routine is set, it will become a habit ingrained in you, like brushing your teeth. You will continue to do HFW© Qigong because you can't imagine life without it. This routine will take time to develop, but hopefully, your positive results will motivate you to stick with it.

Once you attain a strong spiritual center, you will experience the difference when you don't maintain it. My graduates say if they stop doing the exercises, they feel more anxious, irritable, short-tempered or depressed.

Let's hear how Jonathan feels when he neglects his practice of Qigong - 1 min.

But the best part, they say, is that as soon as they re-engage (even after a long break), the balanced feeling returns quickly. Before you know it, this will be your new autopilot OS, and everything you do will be a natural extension of these beliefs.

The Return to Your Soul exercise is one that I hope you will frequently use to continually clear emotional clutter, making way for the window to your soul that always knows how to make you feel whole and right. Continue to build the trust with your inner voice that many of us have been conditioned to believe comes from the negative-biased brain.

What does the phrase "All is as it should be" at the end of the Return to Your Soul mean? It means that any experience you have—no matter how difficult—is meant for you and can lead to peace as long as you allow the intelligence of the soul's Qi to guide you.

I am often asked, "*How do you know if it is the soul communicating or if it's just mental or emotional chatter?*" This is simple once we know how to recognize the separate voices of the soul and the mind.

The voice coming from the mind has an intense quality about it, whether in a highly motivational or censorious way. Mental chatter always causes struggle, tension or confusion in the body. The negative self-talk questions and says, "but," "what if," and "no, I can't." When a thought causes your body to feel uncertain or uneasy, it always involves the brain. It's either originating from the brain, or it is trying to dispute the soul's message, which confuses and does not comfort. Sometimes we can also be given a truth that we are not ready to face or deal with. In those cases, the brain fights the truth and causes discomfort.

When your soul speaks, it is the voice of the most reassuring, gentle, kind and supportive cheerleader you will ever have. Its words always make your body feel at peace with a sense of "knowing." With continued practice, the differentiation will become clearer.

Let's hear Ann describe the voice of her brain vs. her soul - 17 sec.

I had a client who, during a Return to Your Soul in Step 2, saw that she needed to divorce her husband. She dropped out of the program suddenly without telling me what had happened. After she divorced her husband several years later, she told me that she had freaked out when she was shown this message, which she knew to be true but could not face at the time. The discomfort she felt had come from the denial in her mind. Years later, she re-joined the program when she was ready to honor her inner voice.

Does this mean you need to act on everything your soul tells you? No, but it is important to honor all communications shown to you—whether it is something you need to change, resolving a conflict or simply acknowledging a revelation. What is shown to you can even be unrelated to the situation you are clearing. It doesn't matter, nor does it need to have logical reasoning. Your spiritual center is simply showing you the next step of your journey.

As you align and balance, you will be guided to future steps. However, you have free will and can choose how to live and pursue what you want when you want. You would never want to be hasty in making any decision from your brain, your heart or your soul. Stay with it; keep asking your soul until you are comfortable and certain that this path is right for you.

Continue to learn to differentiate between what's coming from your brain, heart and soul and, ideally, come to recognize when they are operating in synchrony. Work to hone your internal checks and balances system.

I've had clients get the same nagging communication over and over, but their mind continues to fight the message. If that happens, it may be easier to make small changes in the direction of this message instead of living with the constant nagging feeling. If you don't change anything, the universe will continue to show you in a variety of ways or nudge you to take action. Remember, these actions are meant to improve your life.

I had a client who had a trip planned with his girlfriend. A month before they set off, they broke up. He didn't want to go alone and planned to just forgo the deposit. In his daily Qigong, he kept seeing himself walking through a forest alone. He knew it meant he should go on the trip, but he did not feel up to it and kept fighting it. Finally, on the last day of his cancellation period, he begrudgingly decided to take the trip but was determined to end it early. He ended up rekindling a relationship with a long-lost friend, made a new business connection and met some other great people. He wound up staying the whole time and had one of the best vacations of his life.

What happens if you feel conflicted and still don't have clarity about what the universe is showing you? Don't do anything—continue to do the 3Rs (release, restore and return) until you are ready to act on it. Practice, practice, practice cultivating your Qi and creating free flow. And start acting on small things that come out of Return to Your Soul to build up comfort and learn how your soul communicates with you. As the relationship with your soul matures, the more you will be able to communicate with it and trust it to guide you through an incredible journey. This takes time but will happen with continual open-mindedness and trust in yourself.

The less clutter we have inside of us, the more ways you will receive communications.

One of my clients was very depressed; she had been harboring ill feelings about a past relationship for 14 years. For the first

5 weeks, every time she did Return to Your Soul, she cried and cried. She was surprised at how much darkness she had locked up inside of her. During the sixth week, her depression completely lifted, and the issue she'd been harboring for over 14 years disappeared. She was shocked and couldn't understand how something that had so negatively impacted her all these years could simply vanish without a trace. Thoughts of her former relationship no longer held any significance. After the release of her long-stuck Qi, she was able to appreciate the gentleman she had been seeing for 6 months and enjoy a more fulfilling relationship with him.

My daughter calls Return to Your Soul a fortune-teller. You have this unbelievable tool at your disposal—let it work for you! To get the most out of this tool, it is important to check your brain during all Qigong exercises because the brain will limit your experience by accepting, seeing, feeling and hearing only what it is familiar with. It will not allow the unknown in, which closes off the enormous power of the fourth energy center—the spirit. I recognize that this is the most difficult part, but take the time to stay with this and try it out.

As your spiritual center opens up, I have found writing to be a very useful tool. Keep a diary or journal and begin to write down all the outpourings of visions, thoughts, feelings and sensations that come from this place of knowing. There's no need to edit; just allow it to flow and write down whatever comes to you.

You will be amazed at what comes out of these writings. This is how Heal From Within© was born. I woke up in the middle of the night, every night, for several months, feverishly typing everything that came to me into the one apparatus that was with me at all times, my iPhone. I didn't realize until a month in that I was creating a program.

My entire program was written on my iPhone from 2-6 a.m. every day. My husband would often wake to see me in the middle of the night typing away. Sometimes, I would be in mid-conversation with him and feel inspired to jot something down. I must say my body was completely exhausted by the end of three months, but something great was also born.

Steve Jobs sought spiritual enlightenment in India in the '70s. He became a Buddhist, which helped hone his intuition and greatly influenced his professional life. As he reflects in Walter Isaacson's biography:

"The people in the Indian countryside don't use their intellect like we do, they use their intuition instead, and the intuition is far more developed than in the rest of the world... Intuition is a very powerful thing, more powerful than intellect, in my opinion. That's had a BIG impact on my work. Western rational thought is not an innate human characteristic, it is learned and it is the great achievement of Western civilization. That's the power of intuition and experiential wisdom."

That's balancing both the mind and spirit—and getting them to work together.

Soul Empowerment

I would now like you to listen to a chant that was created by Leontine Hartzell, whom I met during a week-long Master Peng course to become a certified teacher of his Qigong. Each morning Master Peng randomly selected a student to lead the practice. One of these mornings, Leontine introduced herself as a shamanic healer. Instead of doing a Qigong, she told the group she was going to do a chant, accompanied by Nancy Aleo on her singing bowl. I must admit that I was a bit perturbed and thought to myself, "What is this? It's unfamiliar, and I'm not interested in it at all. Sounds weird. If I knew this was coming, I would have stayed in bed." Then I heard my little voice say, "Stay open." So I did.

Within 5 minutes, Leontine's chant lulled me into an out-of-body experience, which had never happened before. I felt myself float out of my body and go into a trance. I don't remember how long I was in this state; it could have been 5 or 30 minutes. Afterwards, I walked over to Leontine, still in a semi-conscious state (almost as if I had no control over my body), and said, "I think you are meant to write a chant for my program." She was stunned and said, "I could, but I don't have a microphone with me."

Well, before I left for the workshop, my tiny voice said, "Bring your microphone." I didn't question it, so I did. Leontine, Nancy and I found a full marble bathroom with the perfect acoustics to record this chant. I didn't tell her much about my program nor which step I was shown that it would be for. After the recording, she said, "This is to help your clients clear away the emotional traumas of their past."

This chant called "Soul Empowerment" will help you remove any internal forces that may be holding you back in life. Allow her chant to guide you into a meditative state to heal your old wounds so you can Return to Your Soul. You can lie down or sit; then close your eyes and do the Qi Breath, open up all the pores of your skin and let the healing in.

<u>Let's heal your past with Soul Empowerment - 9:49 min.</u>

Codes for Step 3 – Self-Empowerment

Use Return to Your Soul and Soul Empowerment to download these codes to the cellular level of your body.

1. I can create my own script in life. I will improve my desired characteristics so I can love myself fully.
2. I will approach each challenge with freedom of choice and change the situation if I can.
3. If I can't change the situation, I will change the way I experience it.
4. I will Release, Restore and Return to create my own script in life.

Chapter 4 – True Happiness

Reminders:

- *Continue doing Return to Your Soul along with Soul Empowerment as often as possible to release the emotional charge from any conflict, past or present.*
- *Remember you are creating positive flow throughout the body.*
- *Continue to build your Qi Quotient by doing I Am Qi along with the basics of Qi Breath and the Personal Space Opening.*

The true meaning of happiness and how to attain it has preoccupied philosophers since the beginning of time. Aristotle noted that happiness is the highest desire and ambition of all human beings. And today, in the 21st century, it's truer than ever. Of course, we all want nothing more than to just be happy, but what does that really mean? What makes a person "happy" varies enormously.

My definition of happiness is an intrinsic state of overall satisfaction with life. More importantly, happiness lies within us and is not dictated by external things (finances, promotions, social status, a bigger house). Unfortunately, we live in a materialistic society that places far more value on material trappings as opposed to what's happening inside of us. This makes it challenging to differentiate what is really important to us and what relationships, jobs, money—you name it—will make us truly happy. With the help of HFW© to connect you back to your center and flow, you will get in touch with what makes YOU thrive and not anybody else.

Material External Influences

The brain is easily influenced by the material world, and advertisers are experts at preying on that to sell their products. This is why we need to park our brains while connecting to our inner selves. As one of my clients remarked, acknowledging her inner voice was the hardest concept for her to grasp because modern society and education have moved us so far away from spirit.

Some people object to checking out their brains, thinking I'm asking them never to use it again, which is impossible no matter how hard we try. I love and use my logical and curious brain all the time. In Chapter 8, once you are operating from a more balanced place, I will reveal how the brain fits in. The brain is an amazing and intelligent center, but not when it has become unbalanced.

It is important to distinguish between what your brain says will make you happy and what your soul knows will make you truly happy. The next 3 chapters will help you reprogram some basic but faulty perceptions that can get in the way of this understanding.

Let's do a simple exercise. Please write down all the things that make you really happy before reading further.

Things that make me happy:

____________________ ____________________

____________________ ____________________

____________________ ____________________

____________________ ____________________

Here are some of the common answers I have received from my clients:

1. Family	9. Being Cared About
2. Loving Partner	10. Good Conversation
3. Music	11. Good Company
4. Reading	12. Massage
5. Movies	13. Good Food
6. Friends	14. Beach
7. Pets	15. Being Understood
8. Recreation	16. Travel

The first misconception that many have is the belief that in order to attain health, happiness and peace, we need to reach a certain level of success, usually in the form of external achievements like money, status, power or material possessions (car, house, clothing).

Some clients prioritize money because they equate wealth with freedom. We, as a society, have convinced ourselves that attaining wealth and status is the key to happiness because more will afford us the time and the resources to pursue what truly makes us happy.

Now let's look at your happy list. Do you see that most of the things on your list, as well as the list above from my previous clients, can be achieved with little or no money?

The need to accumulate wealth and "things" does not free you; it enslaves you.

The reality is that despite us being the most comfortable generation in history, with more conveniences than ever before, all of our resources and devices have caused us to have less time and become increasingly distracted, anxious and unhappy.

According to the NIH, 46% of Americans will meet the criteria for a diagnosable mental health condition sometime in their life, and half of those people will develop such a condition by the age of 14. Why is this surprising when we are encouraged to prize external and material achievements as the most important aspects of life?

Because they are the most visible and often used as a yardstick for success, we measure our worth and happiness based on these achievements. We have, as a society, become fooled into believing that somehow accolades and achievements will give us inner peace and happiness. If we simply look around, we see that great achievements have not brought inner peace to many of the most successful, beautiful and powerful people in the world. Often, it produces the reverse effect.

Once we achieve this state of excellence, attain the perfect weight, get into that great college, make more money or rise in our career—are we really any happier? Do you walk around feeling elated because you got into Harvard, your son is now a doctor or your husband became a partner at Goldman Sachs? Yes, but only for a very short while. We confuse temporary moments of triumph with true happiness. And then we're on to the next thing, quickly seeking to raise the bar and grasp the next golden nugget.

Worse yet, what if we never achieve the external excellence we are striving for? Do we remain miserable forever, chasing unattainable and unrealistic goals? Not to mention that in these modern times, everything is changing at a speed never seen before in history. So, if we continually chase after the newest, latest and greatest, we can never be fully satisfied. Every time we get a new iPhone, a newer, fancier version is already being tested. And we want that new model the minute it comes out, even though our old phone is perfectly fine!

The more money you have, the more "things" you accumulate, and the more you want to acquire, meaning you need to earn more just to maintain your standard of living!

During my twenties, I worked for an investment bank for 3 years. I was making more money than ever before. According to our cultural standards, that should have been the happiest time of my life, yet it was one of the most unhappy. I remember at the end of the first year when my bonus came, and I allowed myself to splurge on a great stereo system. I felt such joy and pride with my luxury purchase. After the joy of acquiring my new possession waned, I realized that I hated my job more than I liked the stereo. I was internally unhappy, and that trumped everything else. I felt tremendous conflict, which does not lead to balance or happiness.

Let's look at the origins of unhappiness by working backwards:

Unhappiness is about feeling negative inside.
Feeling negative is about being conflicted.
Conflicts arise from not meeting expectations.
Expectations come from your beliefs of the way life should be.
And your beliefs come from human-defined** standards and labels.

Please note, the key-word here is human-defined**

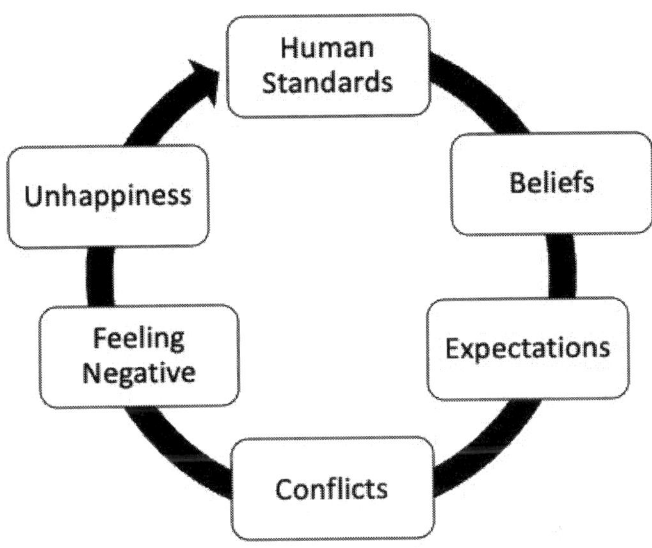

We are constantly measuring ourselves against certain standards, and we feel conflicted and negative if we fall short on any aspect. The labels and expectations that confine you are externally created and conveyed to you subtly and not-so-subtly via the media, your upbringing, culture, and socially defined norms. They all define who you think you should be, how you should look, your behavior, your actions and what you feel entitled to.

Female beauty is something I struggled with for most of my adolescence. The ideal woman has changed over the years, with standards set mostly by men. Today, the standard is thin, buxom and flat-stomached with perfect skin and no cellulite. If you don't meet these standards (and most of us do not), you may feel less-than, unhappy and forever striving to meet this unnatural standard. And what happens if you successfully attain that image? Your momentary triumph will be overshadowed by the focus on maintaining that shape, which becomes increasingly harder with age.

Growing up, I was super-thin, tall and not well-endowed. Quite frankly, I looked like a boy for most of my early childhood. Chinese culture, at that time, preferred a shorter, curvaceous and more buxom look. I often overheard my family and relatives say, "Well … she's not very pretty, but she's smart." I felt fortunate to at least have intelligence on my side. Asian girls, at that time, were not particularly sought after in Levittown. As trends started to evolve … thin, tall Asian women were suddenly in.

Thankfully, I never allowed human-defined trends to determine my self-worth. And once my look was newly "in," I certainly wasn't going to fall into the trap of measuring myself against these fickle standards that I had no control over. Otherwise, I would have forever been enslaved to living up to the current ideal. I did the best I could with what I had and always improved on my strengths.

As we age, our bodies have more ailments and require more time to heal. This is a difficult thing for most people to accept. I often hear my peers, when asked how they are feeling, respond, "Well … you know … I'm getting older and not feeling as spry as I should be." Who is determining that "should be" health standard? It's even harder to accept when we are being brainwashed to believe that aging can be defied.

Our culture's obsession with eternal youth leads us to unrealistic expectations, as we are bombarded with advertisements for creams, face-lifts, botox and other products that promise to make us look younger. We have allowed our thoughts to take instruction from the outside and not from within. You must free yourself once and for all from the confinement of human-defined standards that are constantly and forever changing.

When you die, all attachments and labels are gone, but your soul lives on. The soul does not know who you were, just how you lived. There's a German proverb that says, "The last shirt you have has no pockets." You can't take your material external achievements to the grave … they won't do you any good down there. They're not doing much for you here, either.

Peer pressure has always been a big part of adolescence, but with social media, that pressure has now increased 100-fold. How many friends do we have? How many likes are we getting? Unfortunately, this is what shapes our kids today. Furthermore, young people are experiencing the phenomenon called "imposter syndrome." They are filled with inadequacy and feel fear and self-doubt when they compare themselves to the many curated, flawless and false standards of perfection on social media. And it's not just kids—adults, too, have fallen into this trap.

I remember how hard it was to feel like an outcast for most of my adolescent years. Fortunately, my strong spirit helped me understand that anything I couldn't control was simply a diversion. When people said mean things about me or made fun of me, I asked myself, "Will their remarks help me attain my goals? Will listening to negativity from others help me get what I want out of life?" No, so I didn't listen. I put blinders on and moved forward. I then also asked myself, "What's the best solution for me to reach my goals?" Fortunately, I always heard my wants, values and desires, and only mine.

A defining moment in 12th grade confirmed the trust I had in my inner voice. During a sociology class, I went to the bathroom at the beginning of a lesson. When I came back 10 minutes later, there were 2 lines on the board, and the teacher was asking the students which line was longer.

The next student he asked said, "B," quite confidently. Everybody else quickly agreed that B was longer. When he got to me, I studied the board one last time because I was confused and wondering if I was missing something. Line A definitely looked (marginally) longer to me. I finally said, "Line A," which was the correct answer.

The teacher was furious because I had ruined his demonstration on the power of peer pressure ... a discussion he'd had with my classmates while I was briefly out of the room. He threw the eraser at me and said, "I should have known better than to ask you." I learned a really big lesson that day. *I must always trust myself.*

There's a saying in the finance industry. You are only as good as your last trade. How happy can you be, living under that type of external scrutiny, as well as the mind's ongoing critical self-judgment? Always pushing you to do more: telling you that you are not good enough, you must work harder, don't slow down, you must get this job, contract, raise, etc.

When the external world falls short, you need a retreat that can offset these influences and return you back to self-love and strength. A place inside that you can trust and access easily and tangibly.

> ***"Your time is limited, so don't waste it living someone else's life. Don't be trapped by dogma—which is living with the results of other people's thinking. Don't let the noise of others' opinions drown out your own inner voice. And most important, have the courage to follow your heart and intuition."***
> ***- Steve Jobs***

Self-Defined Box

On top of being affected by numerous external influences, we also wrestle with the negative thoughts that boom inside our heads. This subconscious voice often limits us with self-defined labels that confine us and restrict how we live. Do you have self-limiting labels that confine you (woman, man, LGBTQ, tall, short, disabled)?

Could that label be an inherited trait that runs in the family (alcoholism, mental illness, emotional disorder, genetic illness)? Or a label that resulted from a life event (cancer survivor, abuse survivor, divorced, single parent, adopted)? Many people stay stuck in events that took place far earlier in their lives because the emotional and mental trauma has not been effectively cleared from their bodies. Such labels do not need to define your spirit, even if they limit you in some physical, mental or emotional capacity. When you clear the negative memories (inherited or otherwise) from your body, brain and heart, your spirit can emerge. You can live without labels or boundaries to define you!

When people look at me, they don't see me as the Chinese daughter of alcoholic and schizophrenic parents and the victim of a date rape and childhood sexual assault. They hopefully see my surviving spirit beyond these labels. My cousin reminded me that when I was young, I would say, "I can do anything a boy can do." I wholeheartedly believed that, and still do, but in the feminine spirit that I choose to embody.

The only question is: what does your spirit want to show? Set it free!

Live by Internally Defined Standards

In order to change your relationship with the external world, you must free yourself from expectations. Entitlement is one of the most problematic forms of expectations today: acting as if the world must bend to your wishes and needs. When we live in entitlement, we can become mired in frustration about what we haven't received and try to manipulate outcomes instead of accepting what just is.

Are your own expectations of life limiting you? Can you release your entitlements and just accept... and experience life with no expectations? What you gain will grant you a far richer and more rewarding experience.

This does not mean you cannot have goals. Goals are to set your sights on attaining internal fulfillment, not gaining external gratification for your achievement. When you strive for excellence in the eyes of others, what you really want versus what you think you want can become blurred because of all the brainwashing you are constantly subjected to. What if you continually saw transgender people, plus-sized models and all races and religions living in harmony and thriving in our society? You might start to believe that being true to yourself is enough.

We need to cut the umbilical cord from the brainwashing of the external world. The result is that no matter what happens in the outside world, you have full control over your internal world.

True Happiness Defined

We've talked a lot about what happiness is not and the true way to attain it. The most common answers on the happiness lists give people pleasure and joy—but not true happiness. They are externally driven and will bring momentary contentment. When the experience is over, are you still happy? If you experience a terrible loss, does this mean you are no longer happy?

Remember, true happiness is a state of well-being and content that exists independent of any external source or experience. When you feel this genuine state, it can't be disturbed because it is rooted in internal flow and balance.

This is why in all your Qigong, strive not to be happy but for alignment, flow and balance within yourself and the universe. You will live rich with Qi in an awakened and fulfilled state and direct your external world to match and feed the harmony and peace you feel inside. Instead of the other way around—changing yourself to meet the standards of the external world, which is forever a losing battle.

True happiness comes from an internal balance and strength that allows you to live with meaning, passion and purpose that can't be changed by the direction of the wind.

Molly shares her experience of discovering happiness without even realizing she wasn't happy - 1:42 min.

I've often been asked, how can we be happy and fulfilled when others we love go through hard times. Or when loved ones are sick or dying? Or we're losing someone we love? Of course, these are trying experiences that can make us sad, frustrated or even angry.

These clouds do not need to shroud your entire life. Being aligned with your spiritual center will help you get through the difficult periods, give you perspective and allow you to still see the sunshine in your life. Losses might cause you to grieve for a time, but they cannot affect your self-love, worth and fulfillment, which are the true source of happiness.

So, I hope you realize that internal happiness is something you can't buy or acquire but can only attain through balance in yourself and with the universe. The question, of course, is how.

To stop looking outward for approval or satisfaction means you must start to take instructions from within.

Your ultimate truth comes from your soul because it is the only part of your being that is not influenced by the external material world. This means you need to spend time cultivating your spiritual connection on a daily basis, as you do for your other 3 energy centers.

"Human beings who do not break their self-created boundaries will remain trapped in them." - Sadhguru

Qi Magnet Exercise

You are now going to learn how to influence your internal and external environmental Qi using a "Qi magnet," which will be used in your next Qigong.

Create a qi magnet with your fingers by extending your index and middle finger while tucking your ring finger and pinky under your thumb. Raise the other receiving hand; make sure that hand is upright but relaxed. Point the qi magnet to the receiving hand and picture a lightsaber extending from the fingers to the other hand.

Move your Qi magnet back and forth. Get close to the receiving hand and pull away.

- How does the receiving hand feel?
- What sensations do you notice? Warmth, tingling?
- Do the sensations feel different when you pull away?
- Play with the qi magnets by creating different shapes... circle, reverse the circle, curves.

You can close your eyes to get a stronger sensation.

Let's practice activating your Qi Magnet - 1:34 min.

This is a great exercise to do with a partner. Have the person receiving the Qi close their eyes. Tell them to keep their hands in an upright and relaxed position (not too tight) as you send them Qi in all these configurations with your Qi magnet. Ask them what they feel.

And then close your eyes and become the receiver.

What's interesting is that some people don't necessarily feel the Qi when they do it on themselves, but oftentimes, their partner will feel them transmitting it.

As Master Chunyi Lin says, "If you believe in Qi, it works. If you don't believe in Qi, it still works." Qi is real because energy is real, flowing through us and powering our lives. If you don't feel it yet, you just haven't developed enough sensitivity to be aware of it. Once your brain becomes aware of this life force living inside and all around you, you will be amazed at its power.

Vitality Strengthening Qigong

Vitality Strengthening will strengthen your physical fortitude and self-confidence, which will help you stand strong against the external world.

You will be calling in the energy of the earth for this Qigong. The earth keeps your energy rooted. Without that centering, you are more easily manipulated and influenced by the external world. This is why in most Qigong, you always end by bringing the Qi back to the Lower Dantian, which is at the root of your torso and the source of your grounding, physical energy.

When you bring in the energy of the earth, you just need to picture it in any form that resonates with you . . . a mountain, forest or rock—anything that inspires you to draw physical strength from it. You will then be connecting each dantian, starting at the Lower Dantian, to the earth's energy through a universal force. This higher power that surrounds you will bridge you to earth's Qi.

For me, this higher power is called G-d, but you may call or see this as any strong energy. You are simply acknowledging a higher force assisting you.

This powerful universal force differentiates Qigong from many other forms of meditation. This life force has the power to help and heal us. The X factor of Qigong is to be able to touch this energy.

During a retreat with Master Lin, he invited a group of Buddhist monks at the end to give us a blessing, which was very powerful. And he told us of a discussion he had with these monks, who said in all their years of meditation, they didn't realize that this energy could be used to heal. For them, it was about sharing and teaching love and humanity. Don't ever forget that this is really the huge power of Qigong. When you connect to Qi, it can serve whatever purpose you want, including healing others.

Now, regarding the rotation of the Qi Magnet in this Qigong … it is a left rotation. Always rotate upwards and to the left towards your heart and continue in a circular motion.

Let's build our internal strength with Vitality Strengthening - 8:41 min.

Codes for Step 4 – True Happiness

Use Vitality Strengthening to download these codes to the cellular level of your body.

1. I will cut the umbilical cord from the external brain-washing of human-defined standards.
2. I will not allow a label or identity (inherited or learned) to confine my spirit.
3. I will cultivate my spirit to help me define how I want to live.
4. I will balance my energy centers to cultivate internal happiness.

Chapter 5 – Living in Positive Energy

Reminders:

- *Continue building your Qi Quotient by doing Vitality Strengthening along with the basics of Qi Breath and Personal Space Opening.*
- *Use Return to Your Soul as often as possible to release the emotional charges from old and new conflicts that cause distress and block the positive flow in your body.*

Congratulations, you are now halfway through the book. Hopefully, you are living in a more positive place and handling life and its challenges with more ease and calm. As your work continues, these new practices will also translate to better overall health if they have not already.

For my private clients that have kept up with the program and do Qigong regularly, I notice an energetic shift right about now. Their improved well-being allows them to be more productive and pursue projects that had been put on the back burner due to their health. This is always exciting for me to witness. It is at this point I must also issue a warning. This is where some tend to fall off the Qigong wagon. With their renewed energy, they are able to do more, and the daily meditations and exercises become less of a priority. And as life gets busier, stress sets in again. Without Qi grounding you, all gains will start to dissipate.

The busier you are, and the more chaos is in your life, the faster your fuel burns out. That is why you must make it a priority to continue your Qigong practice daily. In fact, you really need to do Qigong 24 hours a day. I'm joking, but I'm really not. Master Peng told us that when he was training, at one point, his Master Xiao Yao said, "I want you to do Qigong every minute of the day." Master Peng got scared and wondered, *How is that possible?* He went home and thought about it and thought about it. Finally, his master said, "Always connect to your Lower Dantian. That will keep you grounded."

In Heal From Within©, to stay stronger than your stress, you must always connect to the guiding spiritual light in your soul.

Of course, physical health is important, but it is the soul (that lives in the Middle Dantian) that will help you maintain perspective and direct your consciousness in the right direction. That's doing Heal From Within© Qigong 24/7.

Remember that whenever you have 2 opposing forces, the bigger, stronger force wins. This is simple physics. When we are confronted with stressful situations, the one thing we can control is choosing to be the bigger force and refusing to let this situation defeat us. Strengthening your weakest link, which is the spirit for most people, will give you the extra reinforcement you need.

Living in Positive Energy

You've learned that extreme emotions left inside you cause mental and physical blockages. In addition to making you physically ill, they also disrupt your judgment. Remember, we live in a world of energy, and these blockages interrupt the flow inside your body and affect the aura you project—and, thus, everyone you interact with. It's like a pebble dropping into a lake; the tiny splash of water causes a ripple effect, affecting the entire lake and all life within it.

Similarly, as you become more aware of your energetic connection, you can sense anything that interrupts this flow of Qi in and around your body. Let's start to learn how to live with positive energy by processing conflicts instead of trying to avoid feeling negative at any cost.

I have told you why I will never encourage you to "think positively" as a tactic to overcome stress. All the positive thinking in the world can only affect *your* thinking—nobody else's. Maybe, if everyone involved thought the same way, we could guarantee a positive outcome. But that is not how life and relationships work.

So how do you live with positive energy, especially during difficult times? Very simply, by eliminating conflict. Clear away any negative energy, which will then allow you to live in positive energy. It's really that easy!

Steps to Resolving Conflict

When you are conflicted, you feel negative—sad, frustrated or let down—because something or someone (including ourselves) is not meeting your expectations (as I addressed in the last chapter). So let's further explore how to eliminate internal conflict by taking responsibility for your part in any conflict.

- Immediately acknowledge and accept that you feel conflicted. Remember, listen to your body and its warning signals. If the exchange is over and your body still doesn't feel right, or you continue to ruminate about what happened, then conflict still lives inside you. Even if the situation has worked out in your favor, this conflicted feeling may indicate there is something about this situation you are not at peace with.
- Understand your part of the conflict and take the appropriate action to resolve it. For simple conflicts, like hurting someone's feelings or acting badly, undo the wrong by apologizing as soon as possible. This should make you feel better immediately. However, your ego can get the better of you, and you refuse to admit wrongdoing. Qigong will help you soften that dominant ego and give way.

Resolving conflicts can be more challenging when you are dealing with issues that are deeply rooted or complicated by unresolved emotions tucked away deep in your subconscious. Without effective tools to process and transform negative emotions or past experiences, people tend to ignore or repress the pain. These hidden layers can affect your interactions and relationships in many ways, causing conflicts that have deep, tangled roots.

At this point, many of you are probably terrified of the process of peeling back the layers due to the havoc it could wreak on your psyche. No one wants to relive feelings of depression, anxiety and shame. This is why it is important to bypass the brain and work the HFW© 3R process. Release the energetic barriers, restore to an open and clear state and return to your soul, allowing its clarity to see the totality of the situation and lovingly and gently guide you to the root cause of the conflicts.

As you know, learning to let go of the brain to trust, hear, see or feel this other consciousness is where many people have the most difficulty. It is here where I often provide assistance to help clients see beyond the veneer and become aware of underlying personal tension that could be bleeding into their interpersonal relationships. Once identified, they get an immediate sense of knowing, as if the answer has been inside them all along.

If you have difficulty in accessing this other consciousness, you may also get help from trusted and loving friends, family members or therapists who know you on this intimate level. Please remember this is not about heavy psychoanalysis, reliving past traumatic events or beating yourself up about what you may have done wrong. Let HFW© Qi shift the energetic field to soften and transform your intense emotional energy throughout the process. If you feel bad or overwhelmed in any way, your negative brain is taking over, and you must stop and seek help. This is a safe process that is not meant to overwhelm you with negative feelings.

Lastly, act on the personal insights that are revealed to you. Once you act, your internal conflict resolves, and you will feel lighter and more at peace. If you still feel conflicted, continue peeling the layers of the onion by repeating the steps above until you get to the root cause. For deep-rooted issues, this process may take time. As each layer is peeled away, you will see gradual shifts and improvements and gain insights. The end result—a freer you—will be well worth it.

It is important to continually set the regular habit of doing these steps, especially after an upsetting argument or confrontation. A consistent practice prevents you from burying recent conflicts. I'm certainly not saying that you need to do all of this immediately after each and every difficult encounter, as we all have our ways of processing issues, and each situation is different. I have often been accused of releasing my negative feelings too quickly—that is because I dislike feeling pain and suffering. I would much rather clear it and resolve it quickly, so I can enjoy the pleasant sensation of living conflict-free again. You can certainly choose to take the time to sit with, lament over and process a situation. Just don't get stuck there! You can activate the 3R process as soon as you are ready.

My husband was enduring a prolonged health issue, and I was feeling bad about not supporting him in the way he needed. But I didn't tell him right away. I was taking my time to process the situation for a bit. Then I had an incident with a client that caused a distressing knot in my stomach. I didn't feel it was solely my fault, but I did apologize for my part with her (which is all I can do). However, the situation didn't resolve because my client refused to acknowledge her culpability. I was comfortable that I had done all that I could, yet I still didn't feel better.

Then, during a conversation with my husband, I apologized for not supporting him. We talked it through, and almost instantly, the feeling in my stomach disappeared. This is a classic example of refusing to confront a conflict and suppressing your emotions. When something unrelated happened, it caused discomfort that wouldn't go away. As I started peeling the layers of the onion, something hidden surfaced. During that period of conflict, I continued to reflect and used my Qigong to help me shift the energy.

Qigong will help you reach a state of calmness and connection with yourself, which allows information to flow freely through you and resolve internal conflicts more readily.

Let's hear how Jonathan's wife benefited from his improved relationship with himself - 1:55 min.

Forgiveness

The inability to forgive is something that often keeps us internally conflicted, sometimes for a lifetime. For a long time, I thought forgiveness meant that I was excusing the other person's actions. How can you make amends, excuse or see the perpetrator's viewpoint when you can't move beyond your pain? I came to realize that forgiveness is not about the other person. It's about releasing the anger, pain or trauma so it no longer hurts *you.* Once you let go of the hurt, the negative energy released will make you feel many pounds lighter. You can now live in a positive state of being.

I remember two incidents when I allowed forgiveness into my life. The first was a day in my late 20s when I was telling a new friend about some of the traumas in my childhood. As I was talking, I suddenly realized that I no longer felt any anger, bitterness or disappointment towards all my transgressors. I could tell these stories without getting upset at all. I can't explain how this shift happened, but in retrospect, I happened to be in a great place in my life, in control and strong. Being on the top of your game (which was my life's mission) is probably the best remedy to overcome any difficulty in life. Having never really let the turmoil brew inside me allowed this process to happen gradually and naturally.

The second incident concerning forgiveness came during my apprenticeship with Beverly. She taught me that we must be thankful for everything that happens to us (good and bad). She instructed me to thank my dad for all that he did for my family and to forgive him for what he did not. Confronting him was very difficult for me, especially when, in my heart, I didn't feel at all thankful to him.

At the time, my dad's health had really deteriorated from his stroke and Parkinson's, and he was not too lucid. However, when I talked about my childhood and thanked him for all he had done, his eyes lit up, and he gave me a relieved smile. At that moment, all of my lingering negative feelings towards him were released. On both occasions, I felt an immediate lightness in my body and realized what forgiveness meant... and what it felt like.

With the negative energy cleared, I was able to repair my relationship with my dad and see his perspective. However, forgiveness doesn't mean that you need to repair all your relationships. Even though I have forgiven my other perpetrators, I choose not to see or engage with them. More importantly, they no longer haunt me, which allows me to experience life through a different and more enjoyable lens.

Eating

Eating is essential and can provide us with a lot of joy as well as sustenance. Instead, it is a major source of conflict for most Americans today. Today, just thinking about food often comes with negativity and guilt in terms of what we should or shouldn't be eating.

People have become so confused as to what they can eat because so many foods are deemed "bad," such as refined carbs, red meat, sweets, alcohol, mercury-laden fish or gluten. There is no end to dietary restrictions these days.

I first would like to dispel the notion that there is one food that is universally bad or good for everyone. Remember, "One man's meat is another man's poison." This certainly played out in my own family. My middle daughter often complained she wasn't getting enough to eat for breakfast. I didn't understand it because all three were getting the same meal and the same amount. Then one day, I realized she loved meat, something I'd never served for breakfast. Once I started doing so, she felt more energized and satiated. I'd been basically starving her in the morning all those years. She could never be a vegan.

I, on the other hand, have to eat a lighter breakfast to feel my best. The point is that everyone is different. Some people thrive on high-vegetable diets, while others need meat. Knowing what food is good for your body is an exercise I think everyone can learn. One of my favorite ways is an elimination diet. It's like the HFW© 3Rs:

1) Clean out your diet by eating whole foods, no preservatives, no sugar, no alcohol and other common allergic foods.
2) Let the body reset. Hopefully, after the "detox" period, you are feeling better at this point.
3) Return to listening to your body and see how it reacts as you gradually reintroduce each food group back into your system. Your body can and will give you a wealth of information ... when you get back in touch with it and start listening.

We've taken so much enjoyment out of food by reducing it to just how it benefits our physical health. There's a saying in Chinese that food needs to satisfy our hearts as well as our stomachs. If we only satisfy the stomach and do not enjoy our food, it leaves the heart sad.

Sometimes you eat foods that are not good for your stomach, but they make your heart happy. This will only create a single negative. If you then beat yourself up for eating that treat, you are creating what I call a "double-negative" vibration as your body digests the unhealthy food, *and* you feel bad about having eaten it. This is to be avoided at all costs. If you eat that cupcake, enjoy every bite! Savor it and make your heart sing to minimize any additional negative vibrations.

Both negative emotions and food intolerances can affect your ability to digest food properly. Over time, this can lead to severely compromised digestion system. This is why it is important to address both dietary and mental-emotional issues when treating gut health.

Physical Effects of Negative Thoughts

Now that you understand how negative thoughts and conflicts affect your emotional well-being, let's take a look at a few studies that show how this may manifest in the physical body.

A study at UC Berkeley compared 2 groups of mice. Both groups were put on a high-fat diet, but Group A's mice had a full sense of smell, while Group B's mice had lost their sense of smell.

Group A (full sense of smell) weighed twice as much as Group B despite being on the same high-fat diet. Researchers also noticed that the mice in Group B (no sense of smell) had higher levels of noradrenaline, which is a hormone released under stress. This led researchers to believe that this group of mice was stressed due to its loss of smell, contributing to its weight loss.

Similarly, they noted that humans who lose their sense of smell because of an injury, old age or diseases such as Parkinson's often become anorexic. The reason is that loss of smell can lead to depression, which can contribute to a loss of appetite or a release of stress hormones, which affects metabolism. Either way, once a person's mental and emotional health has been destabilized, it can lead to physical and chemical imbalances.

Another compelling example is the research done at the Heart Math Institute showing how thoughts can affect the vital signs of our body.

This chart shows the research that measured people's respiration, heart rate and blood pressure rhythm while evoking negative and positive emotions.

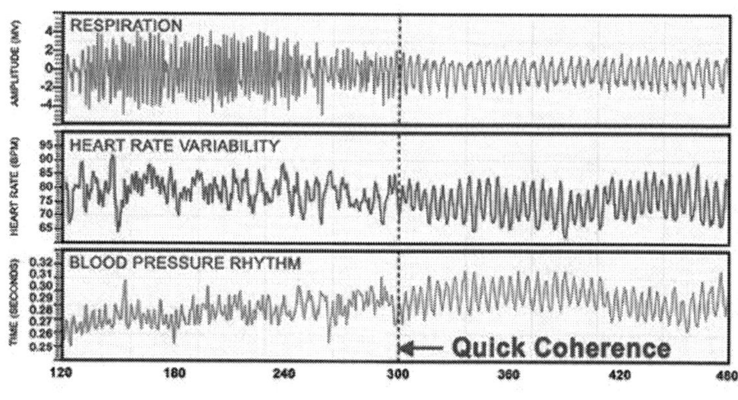

In the first 300 seconds, researchers evoked stress and negative emotions such as anger, frustration and anxiety. Notice the rhythmic patterns are scattered and out of sync. Then the researchers evoked a sustained positive emotion from the subjects, such as appreciation, compassion or love. Their vital signs not only become more harmonious but also more synchronized with one another.

This clearly shows that when an event evokes negative emotions, it causes negative vibrations in the body. How often do we allow these emotions to linger on for months and years, long after the event has passed? We are creating the same negative frequency in the body as if that event was actually still happening.

When this goes on for a prolonged period of time, these negative vibrations can affect your vitals (as we saw above), which can lead to pain and many other ailments in the body. I have a client who emailed me and said she had been on a low dose of blood pressure medication for many years, but after my program, her numbers dropped 30 points. We don't have full control over our health, but it's certainly worthwhile to focus on those things within our control, like our ability to release emotional energy that no longer serves us.

A Word About Pain

Let's talk a little bit about pain and inflammation. I have treated many people who live with unrelenting, chronic pain. So much suffering is a boon to pharmaceutical companies. They produce more potent medications to try to keep up with the pain epidemic, which has led to a serious opioid crisis and increasing drug addiction rates and overdoses.

In 2017, the American College of Physicians released guidelines for treating low back pain, recommending people first try noninvasive therapies like acupuncture, tai chi, chiropractic work, massage and yoga. Many studies show that drug therapies (like steroids) have just not been effective for long-term recovery.

While anti-inflammatories may alleviate pain temporarily, unless the underlying cause of stress and repressed emotions are addressed, the pain and inflammation will persist. This is true for all types of pains and ailments, including those that result from a physical injury. Pent-up stress and emotions constrict flow and exacerbate all pain.

These findings support Dr. John Sarno's theory that psychosomatic responses and emotional stress are the roots of many physical pains. He essentially argues that although people's experience of pain is always real, many cases of chronic pain are all in people's heads and can be better managed with mind-body techniques to release repressed emotions. Using this method, he claimed to be successful in treating 80% of his patients.

If you live in chronic pain and have been chasing an external cure, consider the emotions and events that may be living inside you and contributing to your pain.

Suffering and Double Negative

"Pain is inevitable, suffering is optional." - unknown

Traumatic and painful events are an uncontrollable part of life, but suffering through the misery of them is not. When we focus solely on the pain or fear of what's happening, it only makes things worse. Similar to eating that cupcake, we create a double negative in the body—because not only do we experience the pain or trauma itself, but we also live through the suffering that accompanies it.

The Chinese are known for their stoicism, which has served them well while enduring centuries of hardship and pain. This characteristic helps them to survive difficult times and tolerate discomfort with patience, equanimity and less complaining or whining.

Is this a biological or learned behavior? Growing up, stoicism was ingrained in our culture and simply expected of us, so I believe, for the most part, it is learned. When my kids were young, I didn't give them pain relievers or symptomatic relief for every minor ailment. As a healer, I had many tools that could have continually eased their discomforts. But I felt it was important that they learn to be empowered to not suffer and still thrive by becoming stronger than their pain.

When my kids did not enjoy what they were doing or were in minor physical pain, I did not let them complain. Complaining kept them focused on the difficulties, which exacerbated the pain or hardship in their minds. And what would be worse than raising a complaining child ... winding up with three complaining adults. Raising them to be resilient was of the utmost importance to me.

When my daughter was 12, she had just come home from the hospital after her appendectomy. She was very unhappy and moaning every 5 minutes in discomfort, certainly not displaying any Chinese stoicism. After a half-hour of this, I told her she was only allowed to moan 3 times an hour. At first, she was counting down time between moans, but after the first hour, she didn't make any more noise. She later acknowledged that the moaning made her pain worse.

When you let pain dominate your thoughts and actions, it can prevent you from fully experiencing the beauty and positives of life around us. Can there be great things happening in your life despite your discomfort? Can you enjoy them even if you are uncomfortable? This hyperfocus may also prevent you from seeing the lessons that come from the bumps and bruises in life.

My family was on a day trip hiking in Zion National Park with another family. The 10-year-old girl from the other family was sulking all morning because she wasn't enjoying herself. Then she got wet, and sand stuck to her body. Unfortunately, she didn't have a change of clothes, and there were another 2 hours left on the hike. What started off as a less-than-fun hike had turned even more miserable, and she started crying. Her parents did everything to wipe the sand off, to no avail since there was sand all around us. She kept crying and complaining.

I then had a quick discussion with this girl, asking her to recognize that she had full control over her discomfort—certainly enough that she could at least enjoy the rest of the hike. Or, she could continue to make the whole experience miserable for herself and others. She resisted at first, but at some point, she turned it around and smiled and laughed during the remainder of the hike, despite her discomfort.

To know you have the ability to choose how to react in any situation is incredibly empowering. I want to make sure I stress how important that is. We have full control over how we react... to anything!

When you resist and suffer, you create all-around tension. As mentioned earlier, this interrupts your internal and external flow. When you refuse to accept a situation and continue to fight it, the struggle causes your whole body to tighten. Accepting a situation and choosing to make the best of it will reduce the conflict in your body, allowing it to heal more quickly. Choosing this path also creates an easier mental and emotional experience.

This experience brought me a bit of wisdom that many women will relate to: giving birth. At the end of my second year of acupuncture school, my first daughter was born. I had decided to have a completely natural childbirth without an epidural or pain medication. I have a high threshold for pain and thought, "How bad could it be?" I had it all figured out, or so I thought... since my acupuncture teacher would be there to support me. What was I thinking? The uterus is the largest muscle in the female body, and it was carrying an 8-pound baby.

Needless to say, I regretted that decision after the first 25 hours of the most intense pain that I had endured to date. At that point, I decided to get the epidural. But the doctors said the delivery would probably happen in the next hour, so I decided to hang in there. They were wrong; unfortunately, I was in for another 10 hours of labor. I was so exhausted that I had great difficulty pushing my daughter out, a process which took another

20 excruciating minutes. The birthing process literally wiped me out; it took me months to recuperate.

Two years later, I was about to give birth to my second daughter and had long since decided that this time I would not be a martyr—I was getting the epidural. Around month 7 of my pregnancy, a friend called to tell me about her colleague who was pregnant. Because she had multiple sclerosis, she could not get an epidural. She was going to do something called hypnobirthing, and my friend thought this might be something I would want to explore. Even though my mind was made up to get an epidural, I decided to look into it.

After three sessions with a certified practitioner, I was intrigued. It was time to practice these techniques in real-life situations before the birth. At that time, I was getting pretty bad leg cramps almost nightly. The first night I practiced my new techniques during the cramp, the pain dissipated in about half the usual time—from, say, 10 minutes to about 5. I was encouraged. The second night, the painful cramp stopped even sooner; it went away in about 2-3 minutes. The third and fourth nights were the same. But then a remarkable thing happened: after that, I didn't get another leg cramp for the remainder of my pregnancy.

On my due date, I went to the doctor even though my labor hadn't begun yet, or so I thought. He asked if I had been experiencing contractions or even Braxton-Hicks (the pre-labor or false contractions). I said no. He looked confused and said that I was 6 out of 10 centimeters dilated. I was whisked away to the hospital, where I was immediately hooked up to the fetal monitor. The nurses were astounded at how calm I was despite contractions registering off the charts. They kept asking me if I was fine—and I really was. About 20 minutes before the birth, the pain definitely intensified, but it was nothing I couldn't handle. I literally pushed my daughter out in 2 minutes. Because I had such an easy birthing process, I recovered in no time.

In retrospect, during my first labor, I was in so much pain that I was constantly hunched over, with tension and tightness in every muscle in my body. There's no doubt that my uterus was contracting to push the baby out, but I was compounding the pain by constricting the surrounding muscles. Instead of relaxing and allowing the contractions to do their work, the tension made the uterus muscles work harder with less efficiency. The result: more pain and harder labor.

Resistance constrains your thoughts, emotions and body, creates inefficiency and suffering and weakens your well-being.

Fear is another negative emotion that produces tremendous stress in the body. One of my favorite quotes from Michael J. Fox is:

"If you fear the worst to come and it comes true, you've lived your nightmare twice."

Life and death are the two ends of the spectrum (yang and yin), and one cannot exist without the other. If you spend your life avoiding death, you will also spend it avoiding life.

Sometimes your challenges may last longer than you would like, but this does not mean you need to suffer through them. You still have choices and can learn to go with the flow until you are able to move past it. *The only thing constant in life is change. Nothing ever stays the same!* And until your difficult situation changes, there are still pleasures to be had during times of change and growth. I know this personally; my third daughter was born during my 14-year period of insomnia.

As a healer, many people come to me to be healed, but let's understand that:

Healing comes in all different ways.
When you let go of your conflicts, you are healing your body.
When you love, you are healing.
When you listen to your soul, you are healing.
When you move forward in your truth, you are healing.
When you are unencumbered and have free will,
you are healing.
Start healing yourself by living in the positive.

If you stop the fight and resistance, the healing path will be faster and more enjoyable.

Once you clear conflicts and live in the positive, some of you may feel a void where your negative energy used to live. I know it sounds odd, but it has happened. You don't even realize how much space this energy took up. Many people confuse this high-strung and nervous feeling with productivity. With HFW©, you will never feel a void because doing the Qigong regularly will constantly bring in a flow of positive Qi to keep you in balance.

After the client I mentioned previously cleared her anger, her therapist said she seemed sad and flat. For a time, there was a void where her anger used to reside. Without the Qigong, the mind will fill the void with another negative or obsessive behavior.

Why do I keep stressing that it's important to stop the brain from entering your spiritual center? Because we don't need it in any of the other 3 energy centers. You don't think to activate your 5 bodily senses (hear, feel, see, smell and taste). This happens automatically without conscious thought. An emotion is something that also happens without thought. Love is something you feel. If we have to think hard about who to love and why we love them, something is probably not right.

Similarly, no thought or knowledge will get you back in touch with your soul. What we want instead is to let Qi flow freely and let each energy center express itself effectively and work together harmoniously.

Body Purification Qigong

In this Qigong, we will use the powerful energy of water to flush the impurities out of your body. Water is great for both purifying and rejuvenating. The cleansing effect is also very calming, and many people use this Qigong to fall asleep. There is no movement, and it's a good exercise to practice your Qi breath.

Many clients at this point still visualize Qi, the dantians or organs when meditating. The problem with visualization is we are limiting ourselves to seeing only what we know. And what we know to be the truth today is never final and continually changing. During this Qigong, instead of visualizing, follow your Qi breath and let it lead you to see, feel and experience the unknown truth of tomorrow. This is where the mysteries of life will unfold, and the magic happens.

Let's hear Ann discuss what happened when she stopped visualizing and just started to experience Qi - 2:03 min.

Let's cleanse our physical center with Body Purification - 9:59 min.

Codes for Step 5 – Living in Positive Energy

Use Body Purification to download these codes to the cellular level of your body.

1. I will live in the positive by clearing one conflict at a time.
2. Once cleared, I will fill the void with positive Qi and productive actions.
3. During difficult times, I will avoid the double negative trap. I will stop suffering and resisting.

Chapter 6 – Enjoying Your Journey

Reminders:

- *Continue to detoxify your body with the healing energy of water by doing Body Purification daily… along with the Personal Space Opening.*
- *You can mix and match Qigong exercises depending on what you feel your body needs at the moment. Start with one (such as I Am Qi) and end with another. As always, do Return to Your Soul as often as needed.*
- *During challenging times in your life, your Qigong practice will guide you and help you stay above the waves. Without it, the heaviness can sink you.*

We have all heard that life is about the journey, not the destination, but it can be hard to keep that in mind, especially during difficult times. It is while enduring these challenges that we can remind ourselves of another famous saying: "Man plans, and G-d laughs." There is no doubt some of your best-laid plans have failed to manifest—or worse, backfired spectacularly. To enjoy the journey, we must surf the waves of life instead of fighting the flow. This happens by learning how to stay present, relinquish control and accept what is, allowing life to simply unfold.

Staying Present

Your journey always begins with the present moment, as the present is the only time that really matters. Living in moments that don't exist is one of the biggest impediments to enjoying life's journey, as well as contributing to your overwhelming stress. Let's explore why.

The past is a memory, and the future is an anticipation. You have no control over either of those times because neither exists right now. Living in these nonexistent times does not help you change your past, nor does it create a better present or future.

Your present experiences will soon become your past, so focusing on enjoying your experience now means you are creating good memories. The things you do today will shape your future and hopefully help you grow into the person you were born to become. No matter what is happening in your life right now—whether it's good or bad—the best way to secure a successful future is to succeed in the present.

The experiences and events you are navigating in your life right now are the building blocks to your future. It's just like teaching your children how to deal with smaller issues when they're young. By doing so, children will have the skills and experience needed to handle the bigger problems they'll face when they get older.

Think about it this way:

- How can a child read if they haven't learned the alphabet?

- How can a child have healthy relationships with their spouses, bosses, or friends if they didn't learn how to foster good relationships with their immediate siblings, parents, cousins or grandparents?

As Benjamin Franklin once said, "Don't put off until tomorrow what you can do today." If you move into the future without effectively addressing your current problems, you will eventually have much larger mountains to contend with.

By the time the mountain has become too big to ignore, you may feel like your life is falling apart around you. But the problem is not around you; it's the culmination of unresolved issues living within you. Without this awareness, you may find yourself stuck, spending your time either reliving the good times of yesteryear or dreaming about a better future. If this is a pattern you find yourself engaging in often, employ the 3Rs to free the emotional energy of the past so you can finally address the root issues and begin living in a better present state of being.

Our goal-oriented society makes it hard for us to stay focused on the present moment. We're often encouraged to think about and make plans for the future—one that holds a great deal of uncertainty. This uncertainty and our complete lack of control over what is to come make us anxious and fearful.

When we look at our future goals, we generally view them through the lens of our static present. The inability to see ourselves evolving, which will help us reach these goals, further exacerbates our anxieties. Let's take, for example, a promotion to manager. While this may have been your long-time goal, the new job is stressful at the beginning, given that you haven't worked at this level before and have not yet acquired certain skills and experiences. As time goes by, the anxiety will lessen, and your performance will improve because of the managerial skills you develop along the way. Before you know it, you will master your new job. It will soon be as familiar as your long-time old job! So, if you are looking at future goals, also think about how you will evolve to meet them. However, that is hard to do because we can't foresee all that is still unknown, so this once again brings us right back to staying present.

Many of our dreams and goals are also based on our younger and less-experienced selves. These dreams will likely change as we mature and evolve through the unknown journey that life has in store for us.

In tenth grade, I started thinking about possible careers that would suit me so I could research the colleges that would best support that path. With my limited knowledge of professional careers, I decided that being an accountant would satisfy my love for math and numbers. In twelfth grade, I was enthusiastic at the start of my first accounting class. I was surprised and disappointed to learn that I didn't like accounting, nor was I good at it. I found out as an adult that I have a visual convergence insufficiency, a condition that affects how my eyes work together when focusing on nearby objects. This explained why all those numbers just looked like a meaningless chaotic jumble.

Ask yourself if your life turned out exactly how you imagined it would when you were 10, 18 or 21 years old. If you answered yes, it means that you haven't evolved, that you are the same person you were as a child. Hopefully, you answered no, because you recognize that you, your interests and your situation have grown, evolved and expanded. Your future experiences will shape and lead you to unforeseen paths and destinations. And if you don't get in the way of it, those new destinations and goals will be filled with many rewards.

I'm certainly not saying to avoid striving for or setting goals. It's important to have dreams and make plans that express and reflect the current state of your being. However, make sure you allow for flexibility in your game plan!

Give your dreams and goals room to evolve because they inevitably will. So don't be so rigid and controlling as to accept only one path or outcome. Spending so much energy fixated on your future goals will not improve your present or create better memories. Spending so much time focusing on an uncertain future will instead keep you in a state of anxiety and fear.

All this talk about the benefits of "staying present" is great, but how do you stop your brain from dominating, obsessively thinking about the future and ruminating on the past, all of which keep you in a negative vortex of emotions?

The best solution is to be proactive about something related to the angst that you can control. It can be small! Action makes you productive, helps you stay present and keeps your mind in a place where it can continue to work towards its goals. Even small actions put you back in control.

Here's an example of how this works in my own life. I have, at times, gotten quite anxious about how I will continue to grow my program when it feels like it's going nowhere. My brain won't let it go; I can't stop focusing on it. But I have the tools to manage this state of mind!

1. I do a Qigong to get centered and grounded. As always, my only intent is to clear the energetic charge of anxiety from my body so I can become at peace with my situation. That's it. I do not seek any specific answer.
2. Once I'm in this calm state, I then work on something related to improving my program—market research on the internet, networking or just emailing some contacts, etc.
3. When I perform these small actions, I always feel better because I have taken positive steps towards success and satisfied my brain's need for accomplishment. Try it out.

Approaching life in the present without fear or focusing on the endgame is liberating. This way, you are not a slave to achieving a certain result and can freely make choices as to what feels right to you at each moment. The world can then truly become your oyster.

Acceptance and Expectations

When you're faced with circumstances outside your control, what can you do? Like my childhood. A partner leaving you out of the blue. Getting fired. Such events can certainly make it difficult to face life head-on and endure.

How can you make it easier? By first accepting the situation, you let go of your resistance and become at peace with what is. In calmness and clarity, you can then try to gain an understanding of how to proceed.

When you don't accept, you are refusing to validate what is right in front of you—which is pointless because it's here. This struggle keeps you in a panicked, negative state, which is not ideal when you're trying to come up with a plan.

Please understand that acceptance is very different from saying, "How do I change this situation to meet my expectations?" When things can't be changed, you must figure out a way to be in harmony with your current situation—at least until the situation changes, which is inevitable. Always remember that change is the only constant in life!

Expectations: a strong belief that something will happen because you *deserve* this desired outcome. Setting goals is good, but since we can't control outcomes, it's best to let go of your expectations of how life will play out and learn to swim with the flow. High expectations come with a high probability of not meeting them, leading you to greater disappointments and frustrations.

One day I was coming home from shopping. What is normally a 10-minute drive took 90 long minutes. Preparation for a big parade, along with a couple of accidents and ongoing construction, caused street closures that kept me stuck in endless traffic. I walked into my building and immediately started telling my doorman all about it. He just smiled as I spoke and kept saying, "I know, I know." I was puzzled and asked why he was smiling. He said that not five minutes before, another resident had come in, telling him the exact same thing. But this tenant's story was conveyed a little differently. My neighbor was fuming, arms flailing; every other word was f'ing this and f'ing that. The doorman couldn't believe how I just had gone through the same situation but was smiling and laughing.

This neighbor could clear the emotional charges from his body if he had the right tools. But wouldn't it be better if he could have prevented this over-the-top reaction from building up in the first place by simply accepting and going with the flow? I had woken up that morning with a little crick in my neck, but by noon it was gone. Had I reacted in the same way my neighbor did, I can assure you the crick in my neck would not have healed, and this minor discomfort might possibly have gotten worse. Once again: negative energy has a direct impact on our health ... but it is within our control.

How many of your aches, pains and ailments are exacerbated by your own overreactions or harmful thoughts?

Over-Analysis and Relinquishing Control

Relinquishing control and leaving things to chance is probably the hardest thing to do in our modern society. We believe that if we do enough analysis and make the proper plans, we can ensure the outcome of events in our life. In reality, nothing could be further from the truth. How many times have you done all the research, studied all the reviews and gotten good advice before you act—and it still doesn't work out? And then, at other times, you spontaneously do something that ends up turning out great.

Ask yourself how many times your over-analysis and need for control produced the desired result—I would say probably it's 50/50 at best, but in reality, I believe the number is much lower. Half the time, even though the outcome is positive, the negative effect from the stressful process will live on in you for a long time after all is said and done. The rest of the time, the entire process is negative from start to finish, full of anxiety and ending in failure. This is another good example of a double negative.

Of course, analysis and research are important; as an analyst by nature, I do my fair share. Cross your t's and dot your i's, but let go of the angst and expectations and accept what happens!

Another problem with control is that it leads to a desire for still more control, perpetuating a constant cycle of anxiety. The more you try to control a situation, the more anxious you are about securing a guaranteed outcome.

Control also leaves very little room for the discovery of the unknown. It's important to have unstructured time to offset the regimen of our daily lives. Your spiritual center is a wide-open place where you can let your hair down and be yourself without having to follow any rules or routines. The HFW© Qigong practice is the portal to your spiritual center, where anything goes, and you are free to just "be." Taking the time to explore new thoughts, feelings, experiences and places not yet known will lead you to benefits beyond your imagination.

Allow Your Journey to Lead You

There are times when you do everything possible within your control, yet it still seems that nothing goes your way. No matter how hard you try, it feels like the whole world is set against you succeeding. You continue to try to fit that square peg into the round hole, leaving you tired and frustrated. You may take 1 step forward and 2 steps backward. Or something that has always worked for you no longer seems to, leaving you confused and panicked.

Do you find yourself repeating certain patterns in life? Problems with friendships, coworkers or family members; bad luck just follows you around; or you just can't find love? The ongoing struggle is exhausting and keeps your body in knots. What are you to do in these cases? Surrender. Open up to considering that the journey wants to lead you down a different path. Relinquish control and reflect with a different lens to get back into free flow and harmony with life.

Changing your approach will change the world around you. Learn to let the journey lead you instead of you trying to control your journey. Giving up control is hard, but much easier with HFW© Qigong to soften your dictator brain and allow the soul to give you comfort while exploring new perspectives.

At 32 years old, I left a very lucrative computer consulting practice because I wanted to pursue my passion for health. I was considering medical school when one day, I hurt my back, and my massage therapist suggested I try acupuncture. After becoming an acupuncturist three years later, I was intrigued by the power of Qi and intuitively felt that there was more to it than what the school taught me. I studied with many other teachers and learned advanced energy-needling techniques. Then came my insomniac period, when nothing in Chinese or Western medicine seemed to be helping.

I went outside my comfort zone and sought out other healers, including Beverly, who treated me remotely. This sounded like something out of a sci-fi movie—moving energy without touch and at a long distance. Crazy or not, hers was the only therapy that helped me regain even some of my sleep. Yes, energy can be sent over the airwaves—and at the end of this chapter, you will see that even as a beginner, you can do this too.

This led me to explore other forms of energetic healing and ultimately to the creation of Heal From Within©. With each step I created, I stayed focused on the goal for that particular step without considering where it was going to lead. Something remarkable started happening. In the process of developing each step, I was healing myself on a level deeper than I could have imagined. One step flowed to the next, and by the end, I became more whole, and it seemed like my gears were working together better than ever. That is how I knew the program was meant to come alive.

With each new person enrolled in my program, I stayed present with only one goal: to help that person in front of me. Each and every one of my clients helped me refine the program to where it is today. Had I been more goal-oriented and concerned about this program's future success and acceptance, I might have placed less emphasis on the soul and spirituality aspect, as some suggested, for fear that it wouldn't appeal to the mainstream. Heal From Within© was given to me to bring to life. The more I follow this path, the more enlightened and fulfilled, happier and healthier I become. Being human, even I have deviated from this path unknowingly, and each time my body shows me the consequences with illness and pain.

Let's recap the overview of how to apply the Heal From Within© 3R process when all your tried-and-true methods don't seem to be working out:

At the beginning of your Return to Your Soul or another Qigong of your choice, set the intention of asking to receive insight for help with your situation. Then release the ask and stay present with the 3Rs:

1. Release the negative energetic charge.
2. Restore to a free-flowing state to become at peace with the situation.
3. In this detached state, allow the wisdom of your soul and the universe to arrange the energy and lead you down the path. Be patient and let the insights be revealed to you, and it will take you to a place that is better than anything you could have imagined.

This last part (#3) took me the longest to realize—and still does at times.

Note to self—the sooner you can do this, the quicker you will attain your soul's goal.

When using HFW© Qigong to give you insights on solving problems or conflicts, it is important for the question to be broad. The more pointed the question, the more you are trying to control the process and the less likely you are to hear the true solution you seek. Remember that you have hit a dead end and are seeking help from something greater than what your brain knows.

For example, if relations with your daughter are strained, the ask would be, "How can I improve the relationship with my daughter?" instead of "How can I make my daughter listen to or understand me?"

Trust that every step will lead you to the next. As I finished each step in my program, a quote or writing would magically appear before me in an email, news article or Facebook posting. This poem, which showed up on a social media feed after I wrote this step, sums up this chapter very well.

"Allow" by Danna Faulds
from her book *Go In and In*

There is no controlling life.
Try corralling a lightning bolt,
containing a tornado. Dam a
stream, and it will create a new
channel. Resist, and the tide
will sweep you off your feet.
Allow, and grace will carry
you to higher ground. The only
safety lies in letting it all in –
the wild with the weak; fear,
fantasies, failures and success.
When loss rips off the doors of
the heart, or sadness veils your
vision with despair, practice
becomes simply bearing the truth.
In the choice to let go of your
known way of being, the whole
world is revealed to your new eyes.

Remember that it is your journey itself, not the destination, that will reveal the truth and unbind you from self-created turmoil. The journey is the enlightening part of life; if you allow it to, it will lead you to a great destination.

This journey is not about never feeling pain again. It's about looking at life head-on and accepting all it has to offer. By seeing your experiences as gifts or learning experiences instead of obstacles, you will flow through them much more easily. You will also reap the rewards of endurance, bringing you ever closer to the person you are meant to be.

Stop waiting for the rainbow at the end of the journey—instead, allow your journey to be the rainbow.

Use Your Body to Guide You

Making the right decisions can be difficult. When you are at a crossroads, how do you know if you are to persevere or abandon ship and try something different? Of course, my advice is to always follow your soul's wisdom. But what can you do if you don't hear from your soul? Fortunately, the body has many checks and balances.

Everything you feel and think is reflected in your body. Let the body be your compass. At each moment, do what feels right to you. That will lead you to the right path because right always leads to right. When you act in a conflicted manner that goes against your truth, your whole body feels "off." That's a sign to change your actions. Listen to your body, but remember: we can only sense the truth when we are not in a frenetic state. Always use your Qigong to help you get to a neutral state.

Your journey will not be straightforward, and confirmation of what's right may not come immediately. At each step, keep doing what feels right, and you will reach the place where you need to be, and from there, you'll find your way forward. The soul training exercise outlined in Chapter 2 is also a good way to improve your body's listening skills.

One of my clients, a successful lawyer who worked for the same firm for two decades, had become miserable at her long-time job. During one of her Qigong meditations, she clearly felt that she needed to leave. She found a new job that she was sure was perfect for her. However, once she got there, she realized that it wasn't so perfect after all, and she was disappointed. Had her soul let her down?

I reminded her not to make such quick judgments. Everything happens for a reason, and I urged her to remain open and make the best of her new work situation, which she did. One year later, she landed her dream job—one she acknowledged she would not have gotten without this intermediate position.

It is important to recognize that challenges aren't mistakes, nor are they meant to make you suffer, but rather to help you learn and grow. You may not always be able to see the bigger picture, but by focusing on problems, you become fixated on the wrong part of the story. If you can clear the suffering and see these so-called obstacles as *meant* for you, then you will see their meaning and benefit from them more quickly and clearly.

The most effective way to overcome your challenges is to strive to live in harmony with them. This may seem nearly impossible to do, but it is only when you are at peace that you can begin to see the value of these experiences. Let go of your fears and see your challenges as valuable lessons that can help you grow and get to a better place in life. You might need to change your circumstances or the way you relate to them or simply accept things as they are and find peace within yourself. This is important because if you always look to only change a situation, then you may be missing the real lesson.

Too often, we want to correct a situation so we can go back to our status quo, but challenges are always here to move us forward and not backward.

Why are we so afraid to allow our journey to lead us instead of the other way around? I think it's because we are fearful that one misstep will be detrimental and irreversible. But remember that at each step, you have full control. Continue to listen to your body and act accordingly at each crossroads, and you can never veer too far down the wrong path.

The Drink Experiment

Are you ready to experience the tangible power of your Qi? Before continuing, please make sure you have 2 cups and the smallest bottle of scotch. The cheaper, the better—you just need a very small amount, like an airline bottle. If you don't drink alcohol, please use something like apple juice or iced tea; anything you generally drink is fine.

Let's sense the power of your Qi with this drink experiment together - 5:54 min.

Hopefully, you noticed the remarkable power of your Qi to alter the taste. Your Qi affects and can alter everything you connect to. I have never encountered someone who used scotch in this experiment and didn't taste a noticeable difference. However, if you didn't use scotch, the taste could be more subtle, and you may not taste a significant difference. In this case, please try a different beverage.

Another example of Qi's power can be seen while cooking. Two people can follow the same recipe exactly, yet the two dishes taste different. I have a brisket recipe from the mother of one of my best friends that I make every year for the Jewish holiday. My friend loves it. It tastes *almost* the same as her mom's—with an unquantifiable difference. Your unique Qi makes the difference!

Before continuing to Chapter 7, reflect on the possibilities of how you can use your Qi to improve your life.

Qi Bath Qigong

You may recall that the Central Meridian crosses all three dantians. This powerful energy channel integrates your 3 main energy centers with the expansive and inspiring Heaven Qi and the grounding and maternal Earth Qi. Qi Bath will help you resonate on the same frequency as your universe.

At the end of Qi Bath, you will place your hands on your Lower Dantian while allowing your Qi to settle. Place one palm on top of the other and gently interlock your thumbs. This allows them to be supported and relaxed as you rest them on your lower abdomen.

What is the purpose of allowing your Qi to settle at the end of this and all Qigong exercises? After you've worked at bringing the Qi in, you now want to settle back and allow the Qi to do its job.

Let's do a full body tune-up with Qi Bath - 8:56 min.

Codes for Step 6 - Enjoying Your Journey

Use Qi Bath to download these codes to the cellular level of your body.

1. I will stop spending my time in the past and future.
2. I will accept my present and release control of my journey.
3. I will allow and embrace my evolution.

Chapter 7 – Living in Universal Balance

Reminders:

- *Do Qi Bath daily to open up your Central Meridian and create a clear roadway that connects all your energy centers.*
- *Create a daily spiritual habit of connecting to your Qi and soul.*

In the previous 6 chapters, the focus has been on balancing your internal energies and flow to promote overall well-being. You have worked on changing your internal perspective to get out of your own way so you can create a harmonious environment to reap maximum benefits from the intelligence of your Qi. At this point of the program, most of my clients have started to feel noticeably better as they begin to tap into their inner strength.

One of my clients suffered from severe anxiety about her health and COVID, which landed her in the ER a few times. Every week after our class sessions, she would say, "It is not working," but she diligently continued to practice. Around week 5, I began to hear less negative feedback. By week 7, when she said nothing during our class discussion, I asked her directly, "How is it going?" She was hesitant to admit she was getting better, for fear these improvements would be fleeting. She then informed me that she was going on a trip to California (at the height of the pandemic there) with her husband and two unvaccinated kids. This is a trip she couldn't have even dreamed was a possibility only 7 short weeks earlier.

I hope this is your experience, too; however, if you are not starting to feel better, it is always from not doing Qigong regularly or properly. Qigong is like eating: without it, you will feel weak and malnourished. When you bring in Qi on a regular basis, you feel better because your body is getting what it needs. Without consistent Qigong, you will feel frazzled and less centered, and any improvements will be spotty. I have not met one person to date who has done Qigong regularly and does not feel better because of it.

If you have been engaged in a daily Qigong practice and see some changes for the better but are still not "feeling" the Qi as much as you would like, my educated guess is you are still too cerebral about the process. You may be preoccupied or questioning what you should be feeling as opposed to simply accepting whatever you feel. I had a client who would say she could feel the expansion of her lungs, but that's just air. Or she would feel tingling sensations, but she'd felt them while doing other forms of exercise. I would say, "That is Qi, and doesn't it feel great?" But she continued to ask me what else or more she should feel.

Feeling Qi move through your body—whether it's in the form of air, electrical sensations, or heat—is a great start and plenty of progress for now. Trust in Qi will help you feel more sensations and allow them to benefit you more.

Continue to check your brain during the Qigong and just experience the wow of these internal sensations. In the next chapter, we will further analyze why your head has no place in the spiritual center and will limit your ability to receive its wisdom and benefits.

Try doing some live Qigong classes in person or online. A seasoned Qigong practitioner can greatly enhance your progress by making some minor adjustments in your practice. Their energy can also create a harmonious energetic space that will lull you into a zen state more quickly and with less effort. As long as I'm around, I will be teaching, so join me wherever I am.

Since none of us live in an isolated petri dish, we must also strive to live in alignment with our surrounding energies. Without that, our efforts for wellness will be arduous, like swimming upstream.

Learning self-care techniques in an idyllic retreat is great and can offer a restorative and necessary reprieve from our hectic lives. But how beneficial is a "getaway" if we can't apply what we learned when we're back at home with our real-life everyday distractions like cell phones, work, kids, aging parents, school, health issues... The real world is where I choose to live! It serves as one big live laboratory, allowing me to test and create techniques that work "in real life."

Here's how HFW© has helped Audrey become a better mother to her 2 boys - 1:21 min.

To begin living in balance with your external world, let's start by understanding the fundamentals of balancing yin and yang, according to the Chinese.

Yin-Yang Relationship

Balance is a constantly evolving state. We can never live in a perpetual state of balance because we are continually buffeted by external forces that are not within our control. Life is dynamic and always moving, so the only control we have is to *strive* to live in alignment with the present moment and whatever life throws at us.

The Taiji Yin-Yang symbol is a representation of the balance between two opposing forces that need each other to exist, much like how night and day are two parts of one rotation of the earth. The Yin half of the symbol is black, representing feminine and nourishment, while the Yang half is white, representing masculine and vibrancy. This symbol represents the complete energy that ebbs and flows in nature. To achieve daily balance, you can strive to align your yang (exercise, work and production) and yin (rest, relaxation and sleep) activities with the sun and moon cycle, respectively.

In these times when so many people have insomnia issues and are constantly sleep-deprived, we must recognize the importance of sleep. Our bodies need it to rejuvenate and rebuild from the bombardment of stress and toxicity we encounter daily. This is especially important during challenging times when sleep seems to be the first thing that gets sacrificed. This is largely due to our yang-treasuring society that focuses more on expending energy instead of conserving and cultivating our yin.

Without the adequate replenishment of yin, you will use more energy than your expendable Qi. This leaves you borrowing energy from the other parts of your body (organs, muscles, bones) and puts you into energetic debt, just like when you spend more money than your disposable income and keep charging on credit cards.

In the Taiji Yin-Yang symbol, the dot within each of the opposing teardrops shows that there's always yin within yang and yang within yin. This symbolizes that there is no absolute yin or yang, indicating that there is no absolute black or white in life, and that everything is relative. The characteristics are defined relative to each other. For example, Qigong would be considered a yin practice in comparison to running or swimming. Within Qigong, the movements would be more yang relative to its yin counterpart of sitting in awareness. Both are equally important to provide balance.

In Qi Breath, the inhale is considered yang because we are actively bringing in the Qi, and the exhale is yin because we allow it to passively nourish the body.

Let's examine why balance is so important in our day-to-day life.

Eating has become an increasingly analytical and controlled process. We analyze our food and take more nutritional supplements than ever before, yet Americans keep getting heavier, and diabetes is on the rise. The American Heart Association says that 45% of the U.S. population could suffer from cardiovascular disease by the year 2035.

The notion of balance in Chinese culture applies to every aspect of life, including eating a balanced diet without the need to micromanage calories, food categories, vitamins, minerals, etc. I have to wonder: Could eating a balanced diet that's as close as possible to its natural form without all this highly controlled analysis possibly make our national health trends any worse?

Balance means a life full of varied activities and interests; let's not place all our energy into one basket. We can have many baskets that satisfy the full spectrum of our being. We have work, spouse, kids, home, pets, friends, leisure time, hobbies, etc. What happens if someone predominantly focuses their energy on one area, like workaholics? This will eventually lead to deleterious effects on the other neglected aspects of their well-being and relationships.

Similarly, diversity is an important aspect of building a profitable investment portfolio. When one investment doesn't perform well, your whole portfolio does not collapse. An interviewer once asked Richard Branson, who owns 250 businesses, why he has so many. He said, "When one fails, I have 249 more."

Living life in balance is not only fulfilling, but when one aspect of your life is not going well, you have the support of the other healthier ones. Having all 4 energy centers working is better than 3!

Living in Awareness

Awareness is a central part of living in balance with the universe. By becoming more aware of the most obvious interrelationships of life, you allow yourself to see how you fit into the universe. When you start to see yourself as part of the whole, enlightenment can then begin.

Visualization and focus are impediments to your awareness: both practices have a tendency to control your interpretation of what you see. It's important to be able to see both the known and the mysterious interrelationships of life in the universe, free from the limiting influences of experience or expectations. Open and expansive awareness is the way in which you can experience unity with all things in your universe that science has not yet been able to explain.

All the sensations and visions I receive during my Qigong meditations are born from experiencing them without any interpretation. Where I see purple, others may see pink or blue. This is why I never want to limit someone's unbridled experience by suggesting what they should see, feel or hear.

In HFW© Qigong, your only mission is to be aware of the various sensations happening in your body. Be wowed by all the energy, light, colors and heat you may feel as the Qi contracts, expands, fills, descends and spreads throughout your body. This will allow you to develop awareness through your experiences.

Microcosm of the Universe

You saw in the last chapter how powerful your energy is—you can change the quality of a drink using your Qi.

Hopefully, that has ignited some thoughts on how you can use your Qi to improve the flavor of your life. Let's expand upon this notion to consider the impact your energy can have on those around you.

Everything in the universe is made of matter, including your own body, the earth, and the stars. The same energetic building blocks—atoms, protons, neutrons and electrons—but arranged differently into varying forms.

"Every human being is a reflection of this universe." -Debasish Mridha

A great example of this microcosmic relationship is that our planet is made up of approximately 70% water, just as human bodies are similarly composed of 60% to 80% water. Since ocean tides are caused by the gravitational pull of the sun and the moon, we can deduce that we must also be affected by this energy in terms of cognition, sleep, moods, etc.

Is your brain, lungs, heart, etc., affected by the phases of the moon? Can aligning your energy with this gravity improve your health? Yes! When you vibrate on the same wavelength as the solar system, you have its energy working for you instead of against you. Animals are more attuned to this energy shift than humans because they feel more instinctually rather than intellectually, which is key to their survival.

This notion of a microcosmic relationship is the foundation of Chinese culture, philosophy and medicine. Every aspect (food, healing herbs, exercise) was born from the study of nature's laws, correlating each aspect of our being to the seasons and elements found in nature. In health and treatment of disease, we look to nature as a guide to help us rebalance. The 4 seasons represent the full cycle of life, and striving to live congruently with them harmonizes our energy with the universe.

In autumn, as the days get shorter, we move more towards the Yin's introspective energy. With the weather cooling and the air more drying, we eat foods that moisten our bodies, like honey, pears and seeds. In winter, with the colder, shorter and darker days, we conserve our energy and sleep more to connect more deeply with our inner selves. We eat more substantial and warming foods like beans, meat protein and legumes to supplement us during the cold season.

Spring is an expansive time of Yang's growth and renewal energy. Fertility and ideas germinate from the deep internal connections we made during the winter. We move towards eating lighter meals with leafy vegetables and sprouting foods to assist our growth. Summer is about the vibrant expression of the energy and manifestation of ideas that were born in the spring. With the longer days, we enjoy more sunlight and eat cooling foods like watermelon, cucumbers and lettuce.

Learning to navigate through Yin and Yang while valuing both will help you understand the necessity for complementary forces in order to live a fully expressed life.

Universal Qi

The first law of thermodynamics is that energy cannot be created or destroyed; it can only change forms. This is true only for closed systems such as the universe, where the amount of energy remains constant and cannot be added to or subtracted from. In the same way, the water in the world remains at a constant level despite its changing form during evaporation, condensation and precipitation.

For humans, this means that even though our physical body dies, our energy doesn't. Energy never dies; it gets recycled back into the universe just like water. Every time someone is born, their energy is just recycled from existing energy. This is the circle of life. As an example, let's look at the life cycle of an apple. An apple picked off a tree may seem dead, yet its energy gives us nutrients that help our bodies grow and regenerate. The seeds of that apple then continue to bear more fruit.

The ethereal is not so readily tangible as a piece of fruit we can touch and eat. This is why it eludes and frightens many people. It's natural to fear the unknown. I believe most people fear and struggle with death because they are so attached to their physical form. They believe that when they die, they will disappear without a trace, which is a frightening notion. However, just like an apple, even as our physical form may perish, our energy never dies.

Unlike the universe, humans are an open system, which means your energy exchanges with your surroundings. This is why you can feel and absorb energy from others and your environment. Through Qigong, you can access the vast energy of the universe that is available to us all. This is certainly an exciting notion, one that presents you with unlimited possibilities.

In 2022, the Webb telescope allowed us to travel back in time to get a glimpse of a galaxy when it was created 13 billion years ago. Does this mean that we can connect to the energy of our past to have a say in our present? I believe it does.

Steve Jobs' last words before he died were, "Oh Wow. Oh Wow. Oh Wow." What did he see? Maybe the next stage of his energy? We'll never know, but we can assume it was something unbelievable. I say let's experience the "wow" while we are alive. Although there is truly so much we still don't understand, Qigong can help us connect to the wonders of the ethereal in a way conventional meditation cannot.

Like Qigong, traditional meditation was meant to remove the constraints of the brain and body, allowing practitioners to attain a higher knowledge or spiritual connection. As civilizations advanced, intellectual development superseded spiritual connection. By the late 1950s, meditation began to focus on stress reduction, relaxation and self-improvement instead of spiritual development. Unfortunately, this left us with the current state of conventional meditation practice in western culture. If we are to experience the "wow," we need to go to a celestial space where our brain cannot take us.

Support from the Universe

The role of religion and G-d is declining in our modern society and younger generations, along with our spiritual connection. This has considerable societal consequences and, in my opinion, contributes to more personal hardships and suffering. Without a spiritual connection, the meaning of our existence as it relates to humanity and the world at large is lost.

I believe that G-d is the source of all spirituality and energy, instead of an old being sitting on a throne making judgments on us. If all our energy is connected in the universe, this makes us co-creators of this superior force that we call G-d.

This means you have a lot of say in how your energy commingles with this divine force to make things happen (or not happen). You can feel empowered knowing that you are responsible for how you choose to live your life. Each of us is part of the world, and our energy and actions contribute to the state of the world we all share.

All the spiritual masters I have studied with, including my Qigong masters, have a deep reverence for divinity. It is this belief and the practice of cultivating divine energy that allows Qigong healers to do miraculous things, like healing people from a distance.

The universe is a powerful force that can do great things for you when you're in harmony with it. Understanding how to connect your energy to the divine is essential if you want to benefit from its enormous strength. Master Peng says that when your spirit is in harmony with the universe, you have the universe supporting your actions. Some may call this faith, but faith alone can be hard to trust without feeling a tangible connection to Qi.

Let's hear how connecting to the universe's higher power helped Billy K., a recovering alcoholic and drug addict, to find calm and balance in his life - 3:20 min.

My oldest daughter never believed in G-d, but one day during her freshman year in college, she mentioned the existence of G-d. I was quite surprised. She said, "Mom, nothing can explain all my benefits from the treatments you have given me from afar, so G-d must be real." My hope is that Qigong will make the divine real for you as it did for my daughter.

I would like to introduce you to two short and powerful routines to help you enlist the help of the universal divine energy.

1. First, call in the masters of light for help. You are calling in the energy of masters or experts whom you want to learn from or can assist in the pursuit of your goals. Remember that energy never dies, so those people can be alive or have passed. If you don't have a particular someone in mind, you can always call me in or ask to bring someone in to help you.

   Raise your arms and create a funnel with your hands. Guide the master's energy downward through the funnel to your crown and into your heart. Go into a prayer position and feel that energy go through your entire body, then back through your sternum into your soul. Then thank the masters for blessing you with their love, wisdom and healing to support and assist you throughout the day. End with, "Blessed be they. All is as it should be."

2. Right after, go into a prayer to connect with and elevate to a higher power (G-d or whatever term you feel most comfortable with). Place your prayer hands in front of your sternum (between your breasts). Ask this supreme power to help you get out of your own way, so you can allow this energy to assist you

in achieving your purpose and goals in life. You may also ask for help and healing for others (family, friends, clients) and how you can best support them. At the end of your prayer, always thank this supreme power with "Amen" or "So it is."

Let's learn the powerful Calling In Your Master and Prayer routines - 4:44 min.

During the prayer and Qigong, surrender to the unknown. Let go of what you think you know about your situation, along with any expectations of how you want to receive this help. By letting the unknown in, you are now telling the universe you are open to receiving whatever energy it has to offer. You are willing to align your energy and intention with the Universal Qi.

Let me share a personal story about how powerful the master and prayer routines are. A few years after I had developed my program, I felt there was a new master out there for me to learn from. Every day, in my prayers, I asked the universe to bring me this new master. I started getting all kinds of insights, and I realized I must be channeling someone, but I didn't know who. I kept trying to figure out who this mystery teacher might be.

I kept asking, "What's this person's name?" and saw "Master C," "Kang," and "Chang." What does a normal person do in this age of technology? I Googled masters of a similar name. I finally got a Master Kan from the Kung Fu series with David Carradine. That's when I knew I had to stop Googling and just enjoy this experience.

One day, I saw a post on my friend's Facebook page promoting Spring Forest Qigong. I decided to sign up for Master Chunyi Lin's 6-week online class. The wildest thing is that I somehow already knew everything he taught for the first 4 weeks. It was then I realized the Master C I was channeling was, in fact, Master Chunyi Lin.

It was then that the concept of "the law of attraction" became real to me. It took more than a year for this search to bear fruit and honor my desire. I often questioned why sometimes things could take such a long period of time to manifest. I now believe it's because the frequency is aligned when the timing is right for all. Alternatively, what happens if it never comes to fruition? It is not meant to be, for some reason, which will be revealed to you in due time.

I continue to use these prayer routines for all aspects of my life where I need an expert to assist me. Receiving answers can take time because understanding what is needed to feed your essence and make you whole is an ongoing process. As you become more aware of your true needs, the universe will adjust accordingly.

I've had clients tell me that they've been introduced to doctors and other helpful people who seemed to almost fall from the sky in their time of need. I believe that when the timing is right, the right person will appear. Please always use these routines with pure and good intentions.

When the universe presents you with energy to assist you, be sure to honor it. Even if you are not ready to act, it is important to at least explore what is being shown to you. Otherwise, you are telling the universe that you don't really want it, or you don't trust the information shown to you in these prayers and would prefer to succumb to your dominant brain for answers. This renders the prayers useless, and the universe will stop offering this type of assistance.

Begin to see how your life changes. Continue doing what feels right and follow the Qi. And the more you trust and do not get in the way of this force, the quicker things will happen. The more energy you put towards something, the more benefit you will receive.

My acupuncture teacher was in Colorado taking a graduate course, where he met a fellow acupuncturist whose email address was something like john@lovetoskipowder.com. John skied all the time, and on fresh powder days, he could be found on the slopes instead of at his acupuncture class. It's no surprise that he is a better skier than he is an acupuncturist. The universe will match the energetic frequency to the level of effort you commit.

I don't believe in luck. I believe in energy. If you commit your energy to the negative—whether it's staying stuck in pain, being a victim, complaining or living fearfully—the universe will align with your energy, and you will become the best victim, complainer or fearful person. Remember the law of attraction. If you commit your energy to becoming more peaceful, the best pianist or finding your passion, the universe will show you, and all you need to do is follow it.

The universe will communicate with you in various ways, such as a nagging feeling, an article you come across, a line in a book or a movie, advice from someone, a Facebook posting, etc. Once you encounter it, it will feel "right" and evoke an immediate feeling of certainty. This is your signal for a call to action.

There is great comfort in knowing that there is something bigger than just you out there and that we are all connected. When you can feel connected to the magnitude of our universe, you will treat it with care and naturally live in a magnanimous, charitable and environmentally conscientious manner.

Let's hear how Jonathan's newfound connection to the universe has completely changed his relationship with life - 42 sec.

Universal Connection Qigong

Universal Connection is great for dispersing your energy outward and then bringing back energy that has been empowered by the universe. If you radiate positive energy, it blesses the world, and when the energy returns to you, it will be magnified. If you have an overwhelmingly negative sensation, disperse it outward, and when it returns back to you, it will have been diluted by the positive universal energy.

Think about what happens if we mix a teaspoon of salt in a glass of water. You can't even drink it. How about that teaspoon of salt in a pot of water, a gallon of water, in a pool of water? By the time one spoonful of salt has been diluted in a pool, you can't even taste it. After doing Qigong, people say that their problems can feel a little softer, easier to bear and less overwhelming.

Let's become one with the universe with Universal Connection - 7:26 min.

Codes for Step 7 - Living in Universal Balance

Use Universal Connection to download these codes to the cellular level of your body.

1. I will live life in balance with the Universe.
2. I will empower my Qi and align it with the Universe to make great things happen.

Chapter 8 – Connecting to Your True Self

Reminder:

- *Do Universal Connection daily to allow the power of Universal Qi to help you dilute negativity and replenish your body with the powerful energy from the universe.*

This is one of my favorite moments in the program because it is here that HFW© shows you how to integrate your brain with your spiritual center. You will move from predominantly conscious (or mindful) living to soulful living. Hopefully, during the past 7 chapters, you have felt an internal shift to more calm and peace and less daily stress.

At this point, many of my clients feel a heightened sense of intuition or have begun to receive soul communications (thoughts, sensations and realizations that seem to appear out of nowhere). Some don't necessarily acknowledge these communications because they still credit them to the brain suddenly becoming more aware. These new sensations are signs that the brain is starting to release its iron grip and allow your spiritual center to have more of a say in your life.

Continue this practice, and you will begin to differentiate between the thoughts from the brain, the emotions of the heart and the communications of the soul.

This discernment happens as a result of the most important step of the 3Rs—Return. The Release and Restore steps lead you to the Return, which shifts your mindset towards a more meaningful perspective in life, one that recognizes that honoring your True Self is your ultimate goal. When you live from your soul and the strength of your truth, all that you do, say and feel will emanate from this greatness inside of you. You become an unshakable force! Just like ripples radiate from a pebble tossed into a pond, your energy affects everyone around you.

Self-Confidence and Love

When you are led by your true self, you live with more certainty, self-love and self-confidence. With continual reinforcement of HFW© Qigong, this understanding will be brought down to live at your cellular level. It is here where you can then live by the Heal From Within© motto "Don't Think…Just Be."

Not having to worry about how to behave or what other people think of you is liberating. You may be concerned that acting without thinking may cause you to behave wrongly or in some deviant way. This cannot happen because what comes from the spiritual center is always aligned with universal love and goodness.

Of course, you are human and may not always act from your soul. You may feel conflicted, especially during challenging and confusing times in your life. However, the HFW© tools allow you to continuously return to your soul and recognize when you are not your honorable self. These tools will help you tip the scales to living from your soul's love and confidence more often than not. It is from here that you will make great things happen.

A client, on our 7-year patient-client anniversary, sent me an email: "You have helped me so much with your magical healing, loving advice, support, words of wisdom, your amazing program and more! You have made me believe in myself and given me a quality of life that I could never have achieved without you. You are my earth angel!"

Belief and confidence in yourself are key parts of self-love and a necessity in order to feel in control of your life. Without a strong sense of yourself and your capabilities, you will have difficulty managing the overwhelming stresses in your life and your overall well-being. In other words, things get "out of control."

Historically, society puts us in boxes—trying to sell us the notion that we should all think, act, and eat a certain way in order to achieve happiness and well-being. We are definitely seeing a major shift in the zeitgeist, thanks to all the trailblazers over the years. But these trailblazers endured tremendous struggles to live life as they chose ... as their true authentic selves! Hopefully, HFW© will help you live true to yourself without so much difficulty and trauma.

I struggled with a fear of public speaking all my life. Watching many charismatic speakers present effortlessly without notes worsened my fears, making this seem like an unreachable milestone. How could I share my knowledge with the world without this ability? At some point, my mission became bigger than my fear, and I gradually released this trepidation by using notes to help me present without feeling shame.

A few people commented how they thought I would be more effective if I could learn to drop these notes. I ignored those comments and continued trusting that my energy would transcend this superficial notion and connect with the people I was meant to reach. I may not be the best presenter, but I have something many presenters don't—the ability to teach people how to touch Qi to transform their life.

It felt great to embrace the certainty of my true self to guide me. This does not mean I feel confident and certain of what to do 100% of the time, but even during the times when I'm not, I know how to return to my soul for self-love and strength to get me through shaky times. At the time of this writing, I have gotten more comfortable relying on my notes a little less, but I still use them. Maybe I always will. I take comfort in knowing my Qi transcends it all.

There is no one right way to do anything. I always make sure to tell my clients this because each person is unique, and I want them to trust their bodies and find what works for them. I've been told by many of my clients that having control over the way they practice is liberating because, so often, we're told to follow routines exactly, which can be frustrating when you're trying something new and it is not working for you.

Several clients who have difficulty with the Qi Breath can still enjoy the same benefits as the others by modifying the technique—because they listen to what feels right for them—which, as I will continue to remind you, trumps everything. I have had other clients get discouraged because they don't feel any grand sensations like some others in the group. I always tell them to stop comparing themselves to others and instead become aware of their own positive growth and results.

This is your journey, and if you actively put effort into this work, you'll be in a better place tomorrow than where you are today.

I believe there are three major things that shake our self-confidence in these modern times. The first is fear that's perpetuated by the media's daily barrage of doom and gloom—terrorism, school shootings, the threat of nuclear war and climate disasters. It's hard to live with the constant insecurity of not having control over these random events. But these fears are exacerbated when we start off in a weakened state because of the lack of control over many other aspects of our life—some that we may not even be aware of.

What else strips away our confidence and perpetuates our fears? The feeling of not being able to maintain one's own health without all kinds of help. We all need help, but what if I told you that the more we rely on external forces to keep us healthy, the more depowered we feel? The key to living an empowered life is to have fewer dependencies.

People rely more and more on specialists, medication and supplements to stay healthy. Of course, we all need doctors and medications when we get sick or have an accident, but let's use them as short-term, temporary fixes. Let's manage our health long-term by aiming to empower our bodies back to homeostasis, so we can manage our own well-being and avoid an increasing dependence on doctors and drugs to maintain us for the rest of our lives.

Some conditions require ongoing supplements, medications and therapies, but your goal is to limit such dependencies as much as possible. Work with health experts who can empower you to replace reliance on drugs and medicines with factors within your control (food, exercise, stress reduction, lifestyle). The more factors you can control, the less fear you will live with.

Here's Audrey to tell us how HFW© has helped build her confidence, which has helped her regain control of her health and navigate the medical system - 2:23 min.

As an acupuncturist and energy healer for over 20 years, I am fortunate enough to know that the body naturally wants homeostasis, and we can best assist it by getting out of the way so it can do its job. When the body gets sick, my job is to free the stuck energy and guide it back to flow. I am the catalyst, but the body is doing the work. I just look for the blockage, free it and guide the energy back to balance.

This is similar to raising a child—when a parent takes over tasks a child is capable of doing, they are subconsciously depowering them. Over time, this will add up, and these children run the risk of growing into young adults lacking the confidence to manage their own lives.

The third influence affecting our self-confidence is that many of us believe that other people's opinions count more than our own. We spend more time listening to opinionated programming in the news as opposed to factual reporting because, unfortunately, that's what's being shoved down our throats. We also spend more time on social media admiring the photos of others, observing their opinions and modeling them, which can prevent us from learning what is right for us. By listening to ourselves, we can live in self-empowerment.

When my youngest daughter was 12, she said, "Mom, do you know how I can tell if I forgot to do a part of my homework? I get this nagging, anxious feeling in my body, and then I check my folder. As soon as I finish, the feeling goes away." She is learning to listen to her body and have trust in herself.

I'm hoping that HFW© has started to show you the great power you possess within. The more belief you have in your own ability to maintain your health and state of mind, and the knowledge of what works best for you, the more confident you will feel. This helps you better handle whatever comes your way, including events beyond your control.

Let's hear how HFW© has helped Jonathan regain confidence in being able to manage his life - 31 sec.

Guardian Spirit

Spiritual practices were the basis of all ancient civilizations (Mayans, Greeks, Egyptians, Chinese). We know that nature and celestial studies are the basis of Chinese medicine. Given that many acupuncture points reference spirit along with nature, we know spirit was of great influence in the creation of this healing practice. The reverence for all things spiritual held by the Egyptians is evident in their scriptures and architecture, like the pyramids. I've never been to Egypt, but my father-in-law said to me once… "Siu, if you ever go to Egypt, you will know that man alone could never have built the pyramids!"

Over centuries, we humans began to lose our connection to the spirit. As spiritual practices fell out of favor, they focused more on the physical world and rational sciences. In the late 1800s, psychology was introduced as we learned how to study the mind and emotions. Interestingly enough, the word psychology is derived from the Greek word "psyche," which means soul. Furthermore, Merriam-Webster defines "psyche" as soul or personality. Psychology, as we know it today, has become the study of mental processes, brain functions and behavior, but definitely not the soul. Why did that happen?

It is hard to study something without knowing where it lives in you and how to connect to it. Furthermore, each soul is unique, making it impossible to codify them. Without knowing what influences the soul, it is impossible to research it in a controlled setting. Since we can't train, teach or scientifically prove the existence of the soul, we require a different framework to study it. But the paradigm of Western thought has no infrastructure for that.

Without the ability to intellectualize the spirit, science has continued empowering the manipulatable brain. The more evolved our brains became, the farther we moved away from the spirit until it became nonexistent in both medicine and science.

How can we understand the relationship between these two organs if Western science has no concept of the spiritual realm? If we study spirituality through a scientific paradigm, we will be left frustrated and empty-handed.

A friend told me that he was reading a book on spirituality and children. The first page read, "As I'm doing all this research in my lab. . . ." I said, "Oops, that's the first mistake." Due to the very nature of its existence, the spirit is something that cannot be isolated, controlled or quantified. Each spirit is connected to the universe in a unique way that defies scientific analysis. Since doctors and researchers couldn't find a systematic and logical way to study spirit, they dropped it. Then psychology developed further . . . focusing only on the mind.

Freud then dissected the mind; he claimed it is made up of the id, superego and ego. Again, with no consideration of the spirit or soul. The ego is one of the strongest and most dangerous forces of the almighty brain. The ego mediates your inner world to your outer world, so your ego develops the "I" based on feedback and stimulus from the outside world. This is why the ego can easily become defined by the trappings of the external material world (labels, standards, power).

However, none of these external things feed your essence, which is the core nature and most important qualities of who you are (introvert, extrovert, creative, logical). How do we know? As you have evolved with new labels—earned a college degree, found a new job, married, had kids, made new friends, divorced, relocated to new cities, etc., did the essence of who you are change?

Some clients have disputed this point and said: Yes, I have changed over the years. I have become wiser, less naïve, more active, have more hobbies, etc. These experiences have helped you grow, but they did not change your true nature. Are you competitive, light-hearted, pensive or analytical? What do you like to do when alone? Do you like nature, the beach, mountains or animals? What makes you thrive? None of those changes, irrespective of your life events.

You may broaden your horizons and find more sources to feed your essence, but what needs to be fed and nurtured to make you feel alive does not change. The material things that feed the ego will never define you and feed your essence.

Labels and titles are just placeholders representing all the transitions in your life.

Your ego is greatly influenced by outside forces. Although the ego is usually associated with feelings of superiority, it can also be at work in people who feel victimized. Once the ego stakes its claim to who it believes you are, it aligns itself with anything that supports that claim, whether it is negative or positive.

The ego does not like to be wrong, which is why it's hard to tame it. This stubbornness prevents the ego from exploring outside of its comfort zone. This is why it is critical (once again) to bypass the brain altogether and strengthen the other energy centers—so they can ground and enlighten the ego instead of bowing to it. This maneuver is a key reason for HFW©'s success in transforming mental health.

Now let's discuss what the ego's role is in our intelligence. How does the ego factor into the intellect of our geniuses?

The modern-day definition of genius means exceptional intellectual, creative power or other natural ability. Are we supposed to believe that throughout history, geniuses accomplished what was yet unknown and undiscovered through their own intellectual minds? If we look at the Latin derivation of the word genius, it means "the guardian spirit of a person." A guardian spirit is a supernatural being or a guardian angel. This feels closer to explaining how geniuses like Einstein, Stephen Hawking and Marie Curie could possibly conjure up concepts previously completely unknown to mankind.

The question is, how did these geniuses tap into their guardian spirit? What special qualities did they possess?

Einstein, one of our most brilliant scientists, developed a simple formula that best illustrates the roadblock that prevents many people from tapping into their guardian spirit.

$$\text{Ego} = \frac{1}{\text{Knowledge}}$$

This philosophical formula suggests that the greater your knowledge, the smaller your ego, and the smaller your knowledge, the bigger your ego. *The ego's superiority and dominance limit you from obtaining more knowledge.* It prevents you from exploring outside your comfort zone due to fear of being wrong or failing. This is why you have been asked to set your brain aside during these learning periods.

These geniuses were able to let go of their egos and allow a life force energy in, so they could connect to their guardian spirit to gain more knowledge! This also means that each and every one of us has a guardian spirit that we can tap into by letting go of our egos.

I am pretty strong-minded by nature, and when someone tells me something that's foreign to me, I must admit that my ego's knee-jerk reaction is "no way." But during times of reflection, my ego does soften and gives way to allow for more possibilities. As my Qigong progresses, I can definitively say that my ego has become smaller and more flexible while my guardian spiritual knowledge has become greater.

If you can adopt Einstein's formula into your life—loosening your ego to embrace the quest for knowledge—you will benefit greatly from the doctrines of this program.

Allow the Mind to be of Service to the Soul

What benefit does the ego serve if it is so easily consumed by the material world and doesn't nourish your true essence? Journey the 18 inches from head to spirit to shift the role of your mind and ego to service your true self.

Let the mind and ego be of service to your soul.

Use the brain, body and emotions to carry out your soul's truth. It is my belief that of the 4 energy centers, the spiritual center should lead. Why would I say this?

Why do we want the soul to lead? This idea can be hard to accept because the brain has been in charge for so long.

Right now, your brain may be going crazy because it's losing control. Why is it so important to live from the soul? Because we've already determined that we can't fully trust the mind, too many things can persuade it to do what may not be in the best interest of your well-being.

Just look at the monstrosities created by ego-driven leaders throughout history, such as Idi Amin, Hitler or Mao Zedong. Had they been led by their souls, they could never have caused such offenses to humanity. We never have to worry about our soul because it is always pure and good and cannot be swayed by the external. The only way you can allow the soul to lead is if you can communicate clearly with it... thus, the true aim of HFW©.

Let's change your ego's need from always insisting on being right to simply wanting a positive outcome. This will allow the ego to act in service of a positive pursuit instead of acting at all costs to feed its own superiority. In the end, when the goal becomes realized, the soul is content, and the ego will also feel rewarded.

Abraham Lincoln exemplified this ideology. The book *Team of Rivals* offered many examples of how this President overcame tremendous adversity by forsaking his own ego. He soothed other egos, turned rivals into allies and brought his harshest critics into his administration. In 1864, when he declared his support of emancipation, Lincoln famously declared, "I claim not to have controlled events, but confess plainly that events have controlled me." Not only did he sacrifice his ego, but he allowed his journey to lead him to his ultimate coup with the abolishment of slavery.

In the last year of my dad's life, he had a feeding tube put into his stomach due to his Parkinson's. One of the nurses in his facility gave him medication orally, which landed him in the ER with aspiration pneumonia that almost killed him. One of our aides told us that she had seen the nurse who fed him the medication but did not want me to disclose her as the source. I confronted the nursing supervisor about this incident, and she got very defensive and kicked me out of her office.

During a Return to Your Soul about a completely unrelated situation, I saw the supervisor's face (smiling and with red lipstick). I knew immediately that I needed to make peace with her instead of going for the jugular, even though I was in the right because their careless mistake almost killed my dad. I returned to the nursing home the next week for a meeting that the supervisor was supposed to attend, but she didn't show up. On my way out, she walked into the elevator I was in; she was not happy to see me.

I told her I wanted to clear up the situation and didn't want anyone to get in trouble; I only wanted to make sure this didn't happen again. She went from steam blowing out her ears to thanking me and giving me the nicest smile—one that looked exactly like the image I saw during my Qigong, right down to the shade of lipstick. In the end, the nursing home put new procedures in place so incidents like this couldn't happen again to anyone. My soul was certainly happy, and so were my ego and mind for assisting in producing a great outcome.

Let's take a look at some other visionaries throughout history: Benjamin Franklin, Steve Jobs, Confucius, Oprah and Martin Luther King, Jr., to name just a few. They could not have achieved such success and renown using only their superior brains. If you study the lives of these visionaries, it becomes evident how much each of these very different people was led by their highly-developed spiritual centers. The shame is that our culture leads us to believe that focusing on intellectual development and perseverance is solely what determines success and ingenuity.

This quote is credited to Einstein, who wrote widely on intuition and intellect.

"The intuitive mind is a sacred gift, and the rational mind is a faithful servant. We have created a society that honors the servant and has forgotten the gift."

Unfortunately, more than 60 years have passed since Einstein's death, and his sentiment still holds true. The intuition and spiritual wisdom that guides our leaders needs to be openly acknowledged and applauded. We need to change the tide; let's start by educating the world on the importance of our long-forgotten spiritual center. The spiritual center is where you are both wisest and whole because your soul accepts you, loves you and doesn't know your labels or your identity. It is devoid of the concerns of the material world and always knows what is best for you.

Spend at least 10 minutes every day connecting to your soul because it is a place that feels amazing. It is where you can recalibrate and be shown how to approach life with peace, clarity and wisdom. The more stressed or confused I am, the more I need to practice Qigong. Without it, I get stuck, and my dictator brain takes over, my emotions become heightened, and my body becomes the punching bag. This means that I then have to figure out how to overcome my problems at my weakest point.

When I find it hard to motivate myself to do my Qigong practice, I realize that the internal badgering voice in my brain is trying to dominate. I shift to listening more closely to my comforting soul and not the slave-driving voice in my head that says, "You have more important things to do." All is well again when Qigong returns me to the safest, most loving and wisest spot in my being. Master Peng says that every day you do Qigong will be a good day. I can't promise that, but I will guarantee that every day you do a Qigong will be a better day.

What happens if you let your intuition and spirit lead and the situation doesn't seem to work out well? Does that mean you will not listen to your spirit anymore? Let's give the spiritual center the same respect and latitude as the others. You've certainly had times when your brain was sure this was the right thing to do, but the results were not as you hoped and planned. Do you stop using your brain after such an experience? Of course not. You learn and move forward.

Look at it this way: What happens if you fall in love and your heart gets broken when the relationship ends? Hopefully, you don't give up on your heart or on love. What happens when you overexert your physical capabilities and injure yourself? You don't stop using your body. You rest, recover and keep moving.

My hope is that people do not try to connect to their souls and expect immediate magic. Then, when that doesn't happen, say, *Well, I guess I can't trust my soul.* Why put your spiritual center on a higher level of scrutiny than the other three? Please also remember that progress is not linear, and you may not see how events may ultimately lead you to a better place, like my client, who regretted accepting a position that turned out to be a necessary intermediate step to landing her dream job.

I will caution that if you find yourself repeatedly making mistakes following your soul, it's time to evaluate whether you are, in fact, truly hearing from your soul. Trusting and understanding the truth of these spiritual communications will take time, but it will be worthwhile.

Naming the Entities in Your Four Energy Centers

I would like you to do a powerful exercise that will help you further understand the impact your 4 Energy Centers have in your life. Please assign a label to your brain, heart, body and soul and append your first name to each.

Brain ______________________ *{your first name}*

Heart ______________________ *{your first name}*

Body ______________________ *{your first name}*

Soul ______________________ *{your first name}*

For example, if your name is Linda, your names could be: Brain – OCD Linda, Heart – Honey Linda, Body – Cheeky Linda, Soul – Holy Spirit Linda.

Many of my clients had difficulty naming their soul because they did not have familiarity or a strong relationship with it. This serves as a good exercise to help you recognize which relationships to the energy centers could be improved, as well as the positive and negative impact each entity has on you.

I suggest that you now address your entities by their names when you feel out of control. For example, when the mind can't stop screaming at you, say, "Stop it, OCD Linda, and listen to Holy Spirit Linda." Start to balance the power of your energy centers and observe how their characteristics and your relationship with them evolve over time. Make sure you always say your first name when addressing each entity.

Spiritual Strengthening Qigong

Spiritual Strengthening will strengthen your connection to universal wisdom. The universe holds endless knowledge, and in this Qigong, you are asking it to help expand your personal wisdom stored in the Upper Dantian. I want to differentiate between wisdom and intelligence; intelligence is attaining knowledge and skills through study, whereas wisdom cannot be acquired through conscious learning. It is an intuitive understanding of the workings of the world that can only be acquired through connection, observation and experience.

In this Qigong, you are tapping into the universe, asking it to enlighten you with its vast and powerful source of energy and knowledge. This is similar to Vitality Strengthening, but this time you will bring in the celestial energy of the universe, starting at the Upper Dantian.

This Qigong is a good way to bring clarity and direction into your life when you are confused or at a loss and need wisdom from the universe to light your path.

Let's expand our wisdom with Spiritual Strengthening - 8:50 min.

Codes for Step 8 – Connecting to Your True Self

Use Spiritual Strengthening to download these codes to the cellular level of your body.

1. I will use my mind, ego, body and emotions to service my soul.
2. I will connect to my genius.
3. I will live by this motto: "Don't Think…Just Be."

Mastering this step means that your brain has released its dominating grip, so you are listening to and trusting your soul. When you do this, you will no longer need to strive for peace and happiness because you will be living it.

Chapter 9 - Fulfill Your Destiny

Reminder:

- *Do Spiritual Strengthening daily to absorb the wisdom from the vast universe.*

This moment in the HFW© program is always the most rewarding for me as I have watched my clients transform into a better place. We aren't quite done because there is one more step in this journey to lead you to wake up every day with "joie de vivre." This comes from doing what you love. The common goal for most of the people joining my program was to feel healthier and more empowered, so they could better support their loved ones. When we are spiritually whole, happy and fulfilled, helping others is easier, as it is a natural extension of our humanitarian nature.

We've all heard that the best things in life are free. I hope that now with the invaluable tools of Qigong, you have learned how to bring these free elements into your life and live your best self. No matter where you are or what situation you find yourself in, you can always follow your Qi Breath to bring you home.

Living in Spirit

How will you know that you have successfully installed the HFW© codes into your operating system? You start to live from a less brain-centered, goal-oriented and mind-focused state to a more effortless and spiritual state. You begin to have experiences similar to those of many of my clients: I feel happier even though nothing has really changed, I didn't react while I was watching them tow my car, my energy was able to shift the moods of those around me, people are telling me I look great, younger, calmer or more peaceful, I love and appreciate my family more than ever…

This does not mean that you won't ever have difficult and negative moments, but you will find that as you continue to live and practice HFW©, you will have far fewer of them and be able to get through them faster with fewer bruises. One of my clients commented how this "less bruised" notion could help people prevent PTSD—posttraumatic stress disorder. The applications of this program for shifting energy to improve many aspects of life are vast, and I hope that you will use it and share it in any way that speaks to you.

Another interesting thing I've noticed is that sometimes people aren't conscious of their improvements. That is because our negative experiences continue to dominate and are more deeply etched into our brain more than positive ones. Remember the program goals you wrote down at the beginning of the book? Now is a good time to go back and look at them and compare them to how you feel now. Hopefully, you will have experienced noticeable improvement and feel motivated to continue on this path.

An 83-year-old client came into the program with tremendous fears of becoming incapacitated by a debilitating illness. She believed this came from the trauma endured by her whole family as they watched her mother suffer for years from cancer until her death at age 84. My client was terribly concerned about the burden a disabling illness would put on her own family. At the end of the program, during her exit interview, she said, "As I was coming onto this call, I couldn't even remember why I joined your program! How's that for a testimonial?"

The success of HFW© is due to its ability to shift your energy below the brain's radar on a spiritual and cellular level, so the brain can't sabotage the process. Since the brain's consciousness is not involved in the energy shift, many of my clients cannot explain how it works. They only know that they feel better in so many ways.

I have also had some clients who made great strides despite doing barely any Qigong. They just learned the teachings to reframe their mental perspective. Sadly, the results will be short-lived because these mindful gains always require mental effort. Their "boost" will prove to be just another temporary fix.

When life gets busy and unfortunate things happen beyond your control (illness, family drama, work issues, trauma, death), the brain will become overwhelmed and overburdened, leaving very little mental energy to maintain these new perspectives without the help of the spiritual center. This will keep you constantly putting out fires instead of creating an internal environment so that embers never blaze in the first place. Sadly, this can happen even for my most avid Qigong clients once they stop doing the Qigong and nourishing their souls. They would lose all the gains, just as you would wither away if you stopped eating.

I have seen many people who have daily spiritual practices (yoga, Qigong, religion, meditation), and yet I still see them stressed out and not enjoying particularly healthy, happy or fulfilled lives. Doing a spiritual ritual without allowing the energy to return you to a place of awareness and wholistic perspective is futile. Your spiritual center will not have enough of a say in your life.

Doing a spiritual practice without understanding what it means to live spiritually is living life without awareness.

One of my clients was going in for a major medical procedure. She felt bad that she would need some extra help and require medication to calm her and manage the pain. I told her never to feel bad about requiring external help and to feel grateful that such help is available to her.

She then asked me how I would have handled it. The more difficult the situation, the more I connect to my spirit for help. My brain, heart and body have already given me all they can, so it's time for my spirit to not only take some of the burdens but become the supervisor. A supervisor that can see the bigger picture and put things into perspective for me.

Not to mention that I will enjoy a couple of glasses of wine for some additional external help ... which I don't feel bad about at all.

Here's my variation of Einstein's formula to illustrate the relationship between the brain and spirit:

$$\text{Brain} = \frac{1}{\text{Spirit}}$$

The more your brain is involved, the less you can gain spiritual perspective; the higher your spiritual perspective, the less the brain will control your life. We obviously need to find a balance between the two, and in our brain-dominant society, it's usually the spirit that gets lost. So, if you have been having a difficult time connecting to your spirit, continue to loosen the grip of the brain to give way to your spirit.

Liberation

With all the energy clearing you have done in the past 8 chapters, the luggage of your life's memories will feel lighter. These memories are now past events with little or no emotional charge. You can pick up this luggage, carry it around and unpack it with much greater ease. How will you know you are no longer emotionally burdened? When you can recall or speak about the memories without them evoking an extreme emotional reaction. Of course, the memory may make you appropriately melancholy, but it will not spark heightened negativity nor make you want to run and hide from it.

This is your liberation: knowing that you can choose how to live your life, not as a slave to anyone or any situation, including your brain, body and heart. Being in control of your energy and how you feel, think and act now means the whole universe is open to you. No matter what is going on around you, you can still live in balance. You will no longer try to be the person you want to become—you are the person you were born to be.

Liberation is being able to let go of all that no longer serves you—which paves the way for enlightenment, which simply means attaining greater knowledge and understanding.

Master Peng retells a story from his Master Xiao Yao, about Buddhist Master Foyin and crafty scholar Su Dongpo: Su Dongpo challenged wits with the Master saying, "Master Foyin, people think you are an enlightened monk, but to me, you are just a worthless pile of dung sitting on your pillow all day." The Master replied, "My dear Su Dongpo, to me, you look like a Buddha." Su Dongpo was elated and ran home to tell his sister that he had outsmarted the wise Master Foyin. His sister said, "Oh no, dear brother, you didn't win at all. Don't you know that in Buddhism, the world mirrors the heart? Master Foyin sees you as Buddha because he is Buddha. You see him as a pile of dung, so what does that make you?"

You see in others the reflection of your own thoughts and feelings. At that moment, Su Dongpo became immediately enlightened ... yes, it can happen that quickly. Enlightenment does not require you to spend months or years on top of a mountain. You just need to be open to learning and exploring—and now you can use your Qigong to connect to your genius to experience your enlightenment.

One of my own self-imposed burdens came after becoming a healer and teacher. I didn't realize how responsible I felt for my husband's health. He's had his share of major health problems over the years as a two-time cancer survivor. My Eastern medical beliefs were often met with initial resistance due to his Western beliefs. At times, when my Eastern medicine didn't work for him or he wouldn't follow through, I would feel like I had failed.

I was oblivious to this burden until it was shown to me during a Qigong. Once I recognized this outsized feeling of responsibility I was carrying, I was able to let it go. From that point on, I try to provide the support he wants without needing to force my practices on him. The day after this enlightenment, I felt like I had lost 10 pounds. I was walking to work feeling so carefree ... and again, I didn't understand why until I did another Qigong that day, where my soul was able to connect it to my consciousness.

Enlightenment is a higher knowledge that gives you an intrinsic feeling of lightness and happiness. This feeling is much deeper than anything we can achieve from the external. When I get great feedback from friends, family or clients, it is rewarding, and I do feel proud, but that feeling is short-lived. *One moment of enlightenment is better than all external moments of praise combined!*

External happiness doesn't lighten and free you, whereas intrinsic enlightenment liberates you and produces a lasting change in your life. It makes you realize things about yourself and the world around you that allow for a new, unburdened way of thinking and behaving. I'm human and still have many lessons to learn and *relearn*, as well as enlightenments to experience. I welcome it all in.

Heal From Within© does not take credit for any of the philosophies in this book. There are no new ideas—they have all existed since the beginning of time. This step-by-step guide was developed over years of studying and treating clients and will continue to evolve to help you incorporate these various principles into your own life. However, the true genius of HFW© is its ability to show you how to tangibly connect the energetic dots to live wholly.

Servicing the World

During the writing of the ninth step of my program, I stumbled across an article in *Fortune 500*: "12 Best-Kept Secrets of Successful Business People." The content was not what you would expect to read in a business magazine. I had read other similar articles that made me realize how many successful people and leaders live with a strong spiritual and intuitive sensibility, but teaching others how to do the same remains a challenge.

Two secrets of successful business people that the article listed:

1. They turn to their intuition when making tough decisions. This suggests people can do all the research and analysis possible—and then trust their intuition, which equates to trusting their true selves. The more you believe in yourself, the more control you have over making your goals and dreams come true.
2. They have consistent morning routines. This highlights the importance of starting the day in a calm state to enhance focus and productivity. When you start off rushed and stressed, you spend the day reacting instead of being proactive, which means you are not in control of your day.

This article certainly intrigued me and led me to read the book *Choose Yourself* by James Altucher, the basis of that article. Altucher is an American hedge fund manager, podcaster, author and entrepreneur who started and ran more than 20 companies and sold several of them for huge sums. However, in 2002, he lost everything when the stock market crashed. He got back on his feet but was a physical mess.

Then in 2008, when he had a repeat of 2002 and squandered his latest fortune, something suddenly clicked. He had to figure out how to transform into someone who would not only succeed but thrive from the inside out. He could no longer rely on others. He then made the decision to choose himself by first developing the inner perspective that allowed him to choose himself in the first place.

Alutcher started to build his mental, spiritual, physical and emotional health. He incorporated simple daily routines into his day, including decluttering all his past baggage, emotions and the brain's negativity, staying present, and surrendering to the fact that he couldn't control all the events in his life. Sound familiar? One of my favorite lines in his book was, "Do not give up your Life to live a smaller 'life' ruled by others." He also stressed the importance of sharing your insights and story with others and always remembering to express gratitude.

HFW© is my story that I share with you to help you "choose yourself." Start by living from your true self so you can bring your special talents, gifts and abilities to everything you do. Then share your story to bless others.

Showing gratitude leads you to the ultimate goal of this program. Once you have removed the noise and cleared any conflicts, your soul is guiding you, and you are happy and peaceful. What's next?

Uncover your purpose in life, fulfill your destiny and show gratitude by sharing what you were born to do—to serve others. It is my belief that everyone is put on this earth to make the world a better place by touching as many lives as possible. However, when the mind is stuck and spinning in the daily hamster wheel of work, finances, family responsibilities, health and kids, it's hard to think of others, let alone help them.

The ultimate purpose of HFW© is to teach you how to become the master of your life so you can benefit others.

Back in 2009, Captain "Sully" Sullenberger experienced engine failure on a US Airways flight carrying 155 people, but the veteran pilot was able to safely land the plane in the Hudson River, saving the lives of everyone on board. In an interview, a reporter asked him what experiences in his life had best prepared him to land the plane and handle the situation as well as he did. Captain Sully said, "I feel like my whole life was training me for this one big moment."

I truly feel the same way about my own life, with all its trials and tribulations. However, I believe we all have many moments, not just one. And I'm not done yet.

I had established a successful, busy healing practice, with many people waiting months to see me. When I transitioned my work to incorporate Heal From Within© into my practice, I lost a lot of clients in the process. They weren't ready to go down this particular spiritual path with me. Nonetheless, I had to fulfill my destiny—because when you discover the elixir of life, you need to share it with as many people as possible.

I use my strengths to share my truth to help you discover yours. Now, please do the same. There is no other person in this world with your personality and experiences. Fulfilling your destiny does not require a lot of time spent analyzing or researching.

At the beginning of this book, I asked you to strive for balance, which will naturally lead you to happiness and peace. Fulfilling your destiny isn't about striving for grandness; just be you and let your truth lead and touch others, which will bless many people, including the universe. Serving your purpose in the world will lead you to the most gratifying, empowering, liberating and proud feeling you will ever know.

Continue to employ the 3Rs to lead you back to your soul. Focus on one step at a time, and the journey will lead you to the next step, just like my journey did over 20 years ago when I started with a simple desire to heal others, which then led to studies, many teachers, starting an acupuncture practice, creating the HFW© program and now writing this book.

Warren Buffett, who is one of my heroes, says, "Happiness is being of service to the world." I would tweak that quote a little bit: Be happy within yourself and then share that happiness with others. When you share from your own happy state, the results are much more powerful. And I believe that is how we will support our world and humanity.

As Sadhguru says so wisely, "I'm here to serve life. I don't have a mission of my own."

Ann expresses the importance of HFW©'s work in this world by bringing out the best in people - 1:11 min.

Love Strengthening

When you open up your heart and soul in the Middle Dantian, you allow unconditional love to come in to feed the love inside you. You can then give back to the world with no strings attached, like the sun shining its light equally on everyone. This Qigong is good to use when you feel anger, jealousy or resentment towards others or are unable to forgive or be charitable. Feeding the well of love in your heart will help you to overcome these ill feelings and become more magnanimous.

This is similar to Vitality and Spiritual Strengthening, but this time you will call in someone or something which represents pure love. I chose Guan Yin, the ultimate Buddha of compassion for humanity. You will bring in the loving energy of your choice, starting at your Middle Dantian, where your heart resides.

Let's expand our hearts with Love Strengthening - 8:55 min.

Codes for Step 9 – Fulfill Your Destiny

Use Love Strengthening to download these codes to the cellular level of your body.

1. I will allow my true self to serve my life's mission.
2. I will live in gratitude by sharing my truth to serve others.

The Greatest Love of All

I want to thank you personally for being a part of my journey. We are all connected, and our combined energy makes a more harmonious world possible.

I am here to support you in this journey. Find me online and join my live groups.

I am so excited to see how you will share your story, truth, life experiences and natural gifts to enrich this world.

George Benson's version of the song "The Greatest Love of All" was a hit in the late seventies. A friend dedicated it to me in college, saying it was the perfect song for me. It evokes the true spirit of Heal From Within©, proving it was already percolating inside me even then.

I invite you to find that version and listen to it with hope, then pass it forward to all our future children.

The greatest love of all
Is happening to me
I found the greatest love of all
Inside of me
The greatest love of all
Is easy to achieve
Learning to love yourself
It is the greatest love of all

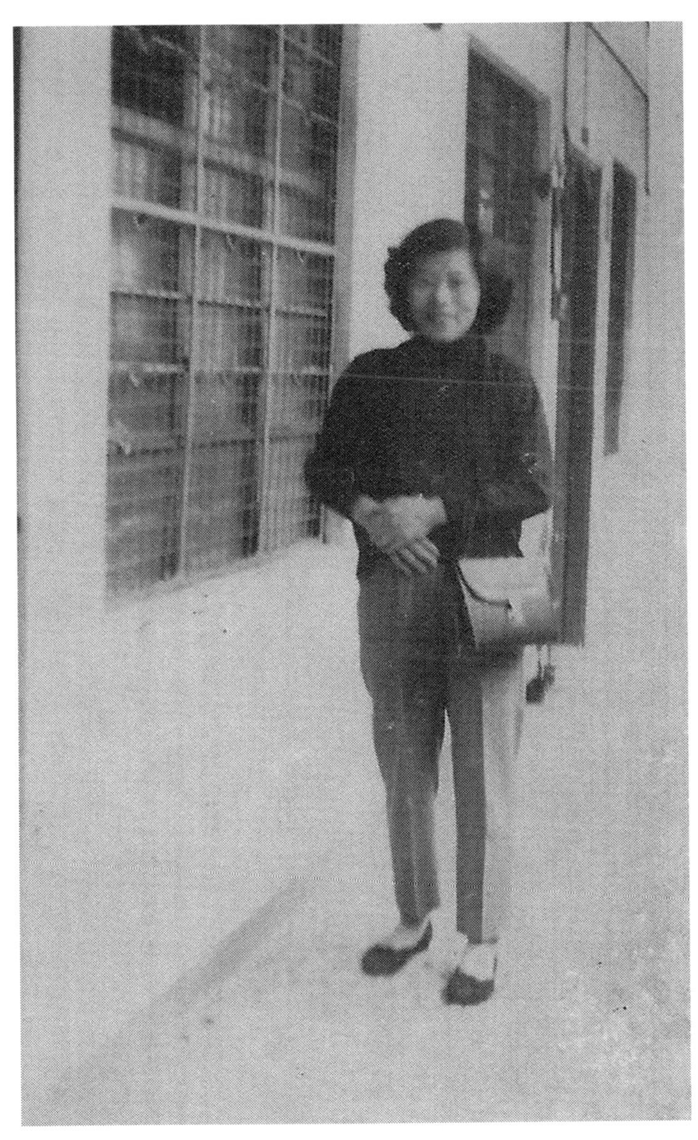

My mother, Yuk Chu Ha, in Hong Kong (date unknown)

From left to right - Me (Siu), my sister Jenny and my brother Kwok Kwong (circa ~1966)

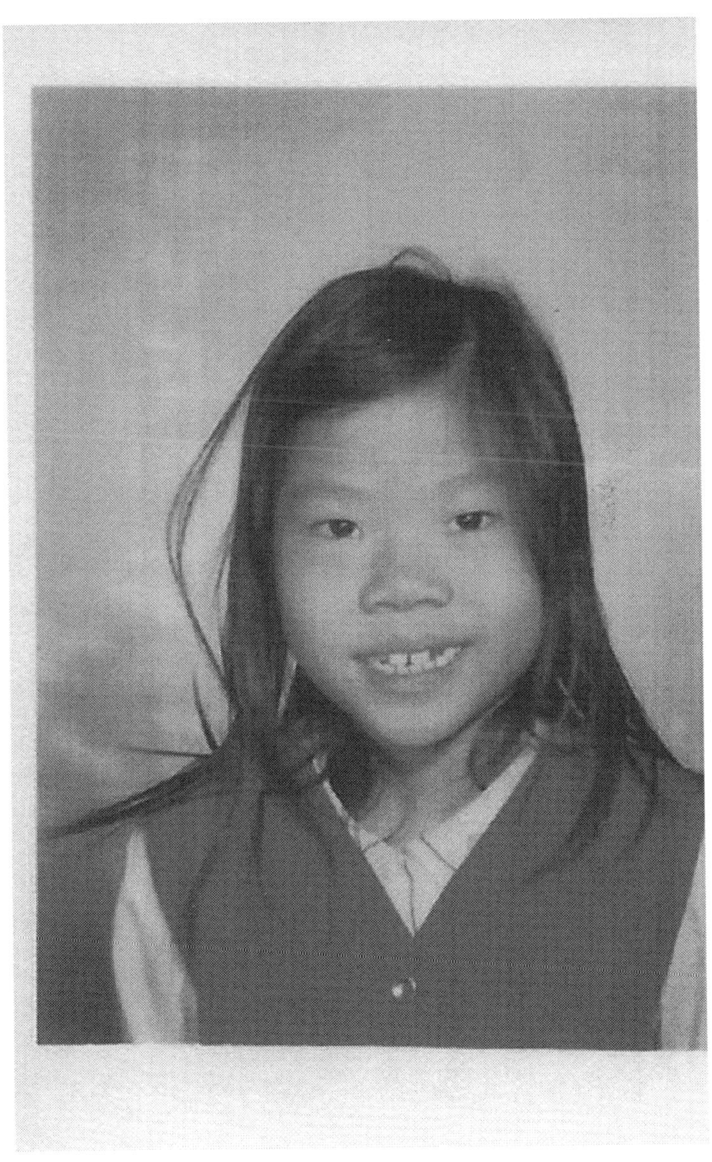

My second-grade school picture

Me and my oldest sister Jenny

My dad, Man Wa Ha, and me at my high school graduation in 1981

From left to right - my 3 daughters - Izzi, Mia and Anna Lei, in Cancun, Mexico

My husband, Renato, and me on our wedding day in 1994

Family vacation in Panama in 2022

A Note to the Reader

Many of my clients watched my online program several times and felt that each viewing helped them absorb the material more profoundly. Some found that they were able to reach higher levels of understanding as each layer of their inner self was revealed. In a world that does not support this type of energetic spiritual work, having the program on hand was a good reminder and support for their spiritual journey. I hope this book will provide you with the same benefits and serve as a useful reference for you to turn to again and again.

I have provided a summary of all the Qigong exercises in this book. The guide defines the original intent of each Qigong. However, Heal From Within© has now been given to you. The Qi is yours to claim to make your own—I don't want to limit you by telling you what it is and how you need to use it. Allow it to bring forth in you whatever it is meant to, in ways I could never have even imagined. Return to Your Soul© is a great example of this. When Master Peng taught me Song Kong Tong, I assume neither he nor his Master Xiao Yao intended for it to be used as a gateway to the soul.

Just like with any exercise program, it is important to incorporate variety. We want to exercise all 4 energy centers and experience the different aspects of Qi. Rotate through the Qigong, and most importantly, listen to your body to help you determine which one is best for you at the time. You can do these Qigong at any time of the day, including nighttime. I like to fill my Qi tank in the morning, so I rarely have to do it at night unless I've had a particularly challenging day. However, some of my clients prefer to wind down this way, so always determine what works best for you.

I invite you to add your own variations to these exercises to suit your needs. The more you do Qigong, the more power is given to it. Just like the chant "OM." Similar to the I Am Qi mantra, it has been repeated countless times; my clients tell me that they feel so much power in just saying the mantra, even without the movements.

Most important of all, continue to do Qigong daily and let your soul lead.

Let's hear Jonathan's final words on how Qigong has become as basic to his survival as eating - 1:17 min.

Intention + Qi (life force) + Action = Mastery of Life

Next Step: A Personalized Transformational Workshop

Siu Ping Negrin's Heal From Within© 9-week online workshop is the next step for those who want to continue their journey of personal transformation by mastering the power of their Qi.

Through live practice and personalized group instruction, my group of teachers and I will dive deep into the book's teachings and tools. You will learn advanced Qi techniques to help you further discover and build a relationship with your soul. Through a variety of different styles of Qigong, you will learn how to put the power of your personal and universal Qi to work for you in daily life. Each week, I offer a powerful healing meditation. You join one of the teachers in this virtual experience, where you will be guided into deep relaxation by using the vast energetic resources of the Universe to bring you into a state of cellular repair and healing. All classes and healings are recorded and available 24/7 to members for viewing at their convenience.

Let's hear how Audrey has benefited from the online group and healings - 1:20 min.

If you wish to embark on this modernized ancient journey with me, rest assured that my 100% happiness guarantee will always be in place. Visit www.strongerthanyourstress.com to learn more about special offers for readers of this book, as well as live events both online and in person.

I look forward to meeting you and helping you unleash the genius in you!

Qigong Summary

1. **I am Qi** (pg 23) - Great way to start your day with self-empowerment by "filling your tank" and aligning your internal Qi with your surroundings.
2. **Return to Your Soul** (pg 42) – Use on an as-needed basis whenever you need to clear heightened emotional energy or ask your soul to provide guidance on any conflict or difficult situation. This exercise is about learning how to create peace and become whole in any situation you are presented with.
3. **Soul Empowerment** (pg 73) - Clear the traumatic emotional energy of your past that is residing in your memory, emotions and body.
4. **Vitality Strengthening** (pg 92) – When you need to strengthen your willpower, determination, grit, courage, energy, fortitude, etc.
5. **Body Purification** (pg 113) – Cleansing negative energy from the body; often used to help people fall asleep.
6. **Qi Bath** (pg 132) – Empowering our spirit with heaven, earth and humanity Qi. Great to do if you're feeling fatigued or need a full-body tune-up.
7. **Universal Connection** (pg 150) – Great to do if you are overwhelmed with negative emotions. Become one with the universe; allow it to dilute the negativity and return perfectly balanced energy back to you.

8. **Spiritual Strengthening** (pg 169) – When you are confused and feel lost, use this to ask the universe's wisdom to support you with comfort, clarity and direction.
9. **Love Strengthening** (pg 182) – When you need to expand your loving spirit to help you acquire patience, charitableness and forgiveness; to let go of jealousy, anger, resentment or other ill feelings towards someone.

Additional Instructional Video Index

Acknowledgments

Having grown up relying mostly on my own strength, love and wisdom, I am most grateful to recognize that G-d was there guiding me all along through this wild journey, bringing me all the influences that made this book possible.

In the human realm, I am grateful for my Dad for moving us to the United States and giving me a life I would not have known and inspiring me to, first and foremost, believe in myself; my Mom for passing down her virtuous traits and fighting spirit to me; my siblings Jenny and Kwok for helping us to stay united against all odds and providing great care to our parents throughout the years.

I am most thankful for my soulmate, Renato, who is my best friend, partner and guinea pig throughout it all and grateful for his belief in me and this program. I'm grateful to my girls—Izzi, for her creative design expertise and the endless support she's given me in all aspects of the development of my program, and Anna Lei, for promoting my health and healing to all her friends. And thank you, Mia, for sacrificing some special Mom moments in order to make this happen.

I will be forever indebted to all my Chinese medicine and spiritual teachers who were instrumental in shaping me into the healer and teacher I am today: Masters Robert Peng and Chunyi Lin for enlightening me about the power of China's greatest secret, Qigong; Andrew Nugent-Head for teaching me the tangibility and movement of Qi; Mark Seem and all my Tri-State College of Acupuncture teachers that started my Chinese medicine journey; Connie Newton, for attuning me to her remarkable Soma Pi healing technique; and Beverly Chapman, for her powerful spiritual teachings.

Thank you to Karen Ammond, my publicist, who encouraged me to write this book and brought every component to my doorstep to help me expand my vision to share and improve lives on a grander scale. Thank you, Julie McCarron, my editor, for your mastery and going above and beyond your call of duty; Bill Gladstone, my publisher, for having enough faith in me to include me in your notable roster of clients; Jaimie Confer, my social media coordinator, for contributing your brilliant artistry to building our online community and my book cover design; Captain Dan Willis for inspiring me as I follow in your footstep and guiding me through the book-publishing process and suggesting the use of QR codes; Gary Rosenberg for your professionalism, expertise and flexibility in creating my stunning book cover and jacket copy; and Chris Knight for your integrity and fastidious final editing of my manuscript.

I am grateful to my colleagues Russell Kordas, Drs. Tom Leung, Dan Wunderlich and Dody Chang, for all the good they do for our Chinese community; Tom, Dan and Russell, for their friendship, professional advice and support throughout my entire career. Thank you, Dan and Tracey Pontarelli, for improving my manuscript with your insightful suggestions; Russell for your numerous contributions in launching my program; and Dody for your thorough reading and editing of my work.

Special thanks to Terri Cole for being an amazing role model and taking time out of her busy schedule to give me advice and support; David and Linda Laundra for all the technical and filming advice that made it easier for me to look and sound my best on camera; Sue Crites and Fabrice Piché for enhancing my online program with their Qigong teachings; Scot Robinson for his friendship and all the technical advice and support throughout the years; and Matt Weiser for his help with all the legal aspects of this project.

Thank you to Stacey Borow, Jennifer Silver, Maria Manuche and Freddie Jeck for their friendship and love over the years; Stacey for her immediate support at the inception of this program and enthusiastic promotion, Maria for your belief in my program and helping me to spread its important message, Jennifer for helping me in any and all aspects that I needed; Freddie, as my biggest advocate and long-standing client, for your steadfast patronage and evolving with me and my work; and Andrea Wolkenberg, for her compassionate care and for being such a great health resource to my family and me.

Much gratitude to Ann Graziosi, Jonathan Szeto, Suzy Nguyen, Molly Bacon, Cindy Casella and Audrey Bellezza, Billy K., Anna-Claire Salama-Caro and Michelle Davidson for publicly sharing your journey to support my program.

Lastly, I would like to acknowledge all my other family, friends and clients who supported my work, placed their trust in me for their healing needs and served as the basis for many of the ideas in the program. A special thanks to all my Heal From Within© clients for taking a leap of faith on this uncharted journey and proving the validity of its formula.

Resources and Suggested Reading

"A New Earth." Webcast Series. Eckhart Tolle with Oprah. Updated January 7, 2018. https://www.youtube.com/playlist?list=PLnYcsBHBvP1-36902GrCQ1eBKiISEmm6x

Altucher, James. *Choose Yourself!* Lioncrest Publishing. 2013.

Brooks, Robert, Ph.D. and Sam Goldstein, Ph.D. *Raising Resilient Children: Fostering Strength, Hope, and Optimism in Your Child.* McGraw Hill. 2002.

Kondo, Marie. *The Life-Changing Magic of Tidying Up: The Japanese Art of Decluttering and Organizing.* Vermillion. 2014.

Lin, Chunyi and Gary Rebstock. *Born A Healer: I Was Born a Healer. You Were Born a Healer, Too!* Spring Forest Qigong Company, Inc. 2019.

Lindbergh, Anne Morrow. *Gift from the Sea.* Pantheon. 1991.

Lipton, Bruce H. Ph.D. *The Biology of Belief: Unleashing the Power of Consciousness, Matter, & Miracles.* Hay House, Inc. 2016.

Peng, Robert and Raphael Nasser. *The Master Key: Qigong Secrets for Vitality, Love, and Wisdom.* Sounds True. 2014.

Sadhguru. *Inner Engineering: A Yogi's Guide to Joy*. Harmony. 2016.

Tolle, Eckhart. *A New Earth: Awakening to Your Life's Purpose.* Penguin. 2008.

Tzu, Lao and Stephen Mitchell. *Tao Te Ching: A New English Version*. Harper Perennial Modern Classics. 2006.

Endnotes

Chapter 1

A landmark 2022 study concluded that antidepressants are not associated with improved quality of life in the long run…

https://www.sciencedaily.com/releases/2022/04/220420151555.htm

Chapter 4

According to the NIH, 46% of Americans will meet the criteria for a diagnosable mental health condition sometime in their life…

https://pubmed.ncbi.nlm.nih.gov/15939837/

Chapter 5

In 2017, the American College of Physicians released guidelines for treating low back pain…

https://www.acponline.org/acp-newsroom/american-college-of-physicians-issues-guideline-for-treating-nonradicular-low-back-pain#:~:text=For%20patients%20with%20chronic%20low,progressive%20relaxation%2C%20electromyography%20biofeedback%2C%20low

Study on the sense of smell and weight loss…

https://news.berkeley.edu/2017/07/05/smelling-your-food-makes-you-fat/#:~:text=After%20UC%20

Berkeley%20researchers%20temporarily,the%20same%20 high%2Dfat%20diet

Thoughts can affect the vital signs of our body…
https://www.heartmath.com/science/

Chapter 7

The American Heart Association says that 45% of the U.S. population could suffer from cardiovascular disease…

https://www.heart.org/en/get-involved/advocate/federal-priorities/cardiovascular-disease-burden-report

Chapter 9

Commentary: 12 best-kept secrets of successful business people…

https://fortune.com/2015/03/13/12-best-kept-secrets-of-successful-business-people/

About the Author

Siu Ping Negrin is a Qigong healer, spiritual coach, licensed acupuncturist and founder of Heal From Within©. She received a Master's in Acupuncture from Tri-State College of Acupuncture with an additional 2-year concentration in Orthopedics and Rehabilitation. She also holds a BS in Applied Mathematics and Computer Science from SUNY Albany. For over 20 years, she has helped clients heal using Chinese medicine (acupuncture, herbs, diet and Qigong) along with other natural modalities, foods, supplements and exercises. She specializes in wholistic healing by treating imbalances of the body that manifest in a wide range of ailments, including musculoskeletal pain, migraines, infertility, gastrointestinal disorders, mental and emotional disorders, cancer, autoimmune, arthritis, stroke and Bell's Palsy.

As a result of her personal battle with insomnia, she now teaches people how to be in control of their energy and provides energy healings (in-person and remotely) to help clients heal and find insights to help them live their personal best in health, happiness and fulfillment. Siu uses her unique approach to wholistic health—combining Chinese medicine with scientific knowledge—to address the impact of modern-day stresses and ailments on the body, mind, emotions and spirit. As an avid student, practitioner and consumer of Chinese medicine, Siu hopes that in her lifetime, this important medical system will be recognized and given parity alongside Western medicine in modern-day healthcare.

Tiktok @siupinghealing
Instagram @siupinghealing
YouTube @siupinghealing
Facebook @siupingheal

Made in the USA
Middletown, DE
09 May 2023

30252898R00137